THE PICTORIAL HISTORY OF
LAND BATTLES

ALASTAIR REVIE

ENIGMA

LAND BATTLES

PICTURES SUPPLIED BY:

Associated Press 90
Bapty & Co. Cover
British Museum Newspaper Library 48, 50, 54
Bundesarchiv; Koblenz 84
Photo Giraudon 32
Robert Hunt Picture Library 4-5
Imperial War Museum 36, 48, 62, 63, 64, 65, 68, 70, 76, 81, 82, 83, 101, 102, 105, 106, 118
Mansell Collection 6, 7, 11, 20, 21(rt), 22, 30, 31, 52, 53
J. G. Moore Collection 14, 15, 36, 41, 46
Musée de Versailles 28-29
National Army Museum 27, 33, 34
Novosti Press Agency 87, 90, 97
National Portrait Gallery 50, 55
Public Archives of Canada 120, 123
RAC Tank Museum 126
Radio Times-Hulton Picture Library 52
Scala, Milan 8-9
M. A. Snelgrove 16-17
Staatsbibliothek 78, 85, 98
Süddeutscher Verlag 60, 66, 72, 76
USAF 105
US Army 100, 103, 108, 112, 117, 124, 125, 128
US National Archives 26, 52, 54, 56, 62, 74, 86, 92, 94
Washington-Lee University 21
Yale University Art Gallery 24
Zeitgeschichtliches Bildarchiv 112-113

Maps by Allard Design Group

Diagrams by James Bamber 60, 61, 69, 81, 88, 90, 91, 103, 104, 116
Tony Bryan 114
Peter Sarson/Tony Bryan 80

Published by Enigma Books Limited,
58 Old Compton Street, London W1V 5PA

© Marshall Cavendish Limited 1974, 1977

First printing 1974
Second printing 1977

Printed in Hong Kong

ISBN 0 85685 076 4

ABOUT THIS BOOK

This is the book you have always wanted,
a book that covers that vast subject—war on land.

From a forced march by Roman legions to
Hitler's fast-moving Panzer troops, from a
sweeping Confederate victory master-minded
by 'Stonewall' Jackson to the mud, blood
and slime of World War I, from the long-bow
to the King Tiger, *The Pictorial History
of Land Battles* is the story of conflict
on land.

For the knowledgeable enthusiast or the
interested tyro, *The Pictorial History of
Land Battles* is your full guide to the most
important battles of all time: why they were
fought, the leaders—and the men—involved,
the tactics and the weapons they used.

The authoritative and highly-readable text
has all the information you require,
specially-drawn maps give you a clear guide
to the action, detailed diagrams flesh out the
technical specifications of guns and tanks and
dozens of illustrations, many in full colour,
bring you the excitement, the danger—and the
sadness—of war.

The Pictorial History of Land Battles
will take you right into the world of the great
generals, the great heroes and the great fighting
machines. Put it on your bookshelf and you
will consult it again and again.

CONTENTS

METAURUS

Rome in 207 B.C. lay open before the Carthaginian armies of Hannibal and Hasdrubal. Yet the Consul Nero out-bluffed Hannibal and then, after the toughest forced march in history, defeated and slew Hasdrubal beside the river Metaurus.

The Romans of classical times were brutal as they were brave. In winning for Rome the most important battle of the two Punic Wars fought against the Carthaginians, their elected consul Gaius Nero not only mercilessly slaughtered the second Carthaginian army on a river bank by the Adriatic in northern Italy; he also hacked off the enemy general's head and carried it on a short-sword to Canusium in the extreme south of the land; and at Canusium, he contemptuously tossed the gory skull into the camp of the first Carthaginian army.

It was one of the most fitting dramatic gestures in military history.

The tousled, glassy-eyed head was that of Hasdrubal.

The camp into which it bounced like a football was the headquarters of Hasdrubal's equally famous brother Hannibal . . . they of the surname Barca, meaning Thunderbolt.

These two sons of Hamilcar the Great, ruthlessly raised, like lions' whelps, had taken a vow at their father's knee to hate Rome and to make war on her, not for prizes but for prestige and revenge. They had succeeded to the point that Hannibal roamed Italy almost at will and brave senators trembled at sight of a double H. Now the tables of power were turned with a vengeance.

Hannibal and Hasdrubal had been about to link armies to crush Rome once and for all, and to make the Punic power supreme over all na-

tions. But Nero's inspired interception had unexpectedly changed history. The Roman Empire was shaking itself free, and it had the will to be great.

As he brushed the matted locks away from the brother's face he had last seen 11 years before, Hannibal wept; and when he raised his head it was to groan aloud in bitterness, saying: 'All is lost. Rome will now be mistress of the world.'

Hannibal comes to Italy

Hannibal had earlier pointed up his greatness in making his incredible elephant march across the Alps in 218 B.C. This had been enterprise and showmanship of the highest order. On its completion, his name rang round the Mediterranean like that of a god.

But the march had also been a grim ploy in which he lost about half his seasoned troops. And the truth was it had been necessary because Carthage no longer commanded the seas.

In the event, it worked wonders. His descent into the heart of Italy, then controlled by the City State of Rome, together with the brilliance of his cavalry-led tactics, enabled him to slaughter two Roman armies, totalling over 100,000 men, and their consuls with them. Thus depleted, the Romans did not dare say boo to him; apart from other factors, about two-thirds of their million troops were 'allies', not always reliable in adversity.

But Hannibal was also fallible; and he made the big mistake (probably because he lacked siege equipment) of not attacking the city of Rome. Instead he chose to impoverish much of Italy and so bankrupt the Romans.

The 'game' between Hannibal and Rome was in many respects the precursor of that between Napoleon and England, with an individual of genius taking on a great power. In both cases, the individual lost the last battle; after 17 years in Hannibal's case; after 16 in Napoleon's.

Yet, as with Napoleon, Hannibal's thirst for satisfaction was never even temporarily quenched, for the Roman Republic's Senate magnificently refused to accept the true situation.

Left The ancient 'tank' against Roman legionaries. To disable it either the underbelly had to be stabbed or the legs hamstrung. It might, however, panic anyway.

The stern spirit of Roman resolution was ever highest in adversity or danger.

Hasdrubal follows Hannibal

While Hannibal rampaged Italy, his brother Hasdrubal had been engaging the Romans in Spain, and had then followed his brother's ploy by marching his elephants, horses and men across the Pyrenees and the Alps. His route was surer and his losses were smaller; indeed, he was able to gather strength, every league of his journey, in recruits from among the mountain tribes, attracted by the high rates of pay he offered.

Hasdrubal's 50,000 were also speeded by the excellence of the engineering works Hannibal's experts had laid; in due course, they emerged

Below Nero made the savage gesture of throwing Hasdrubal's head into the camp of Hannibal, his elder brother, on a night six days after the battle.
Overleaf Africanus confronts Hannibal across a river five years after Metaurus where the consul Nero defeated Hasdrubal, Hannibal's brother, and destroyed Hannibal's last hope of victory in Italy. The Carthaginian was forced to return home in 202 B.C.

SCIPIO ET ANNIBAL
SVPER PA...A
AD INVICEM
CONVENIVNT

from the Alpine valleys much sooner than had been anticipated. They crossed the Po in good weather and advanced beyond Ariminum on the Adriatic, over the Metaurus, and as far as the little town of Sena to the south-east of that river (not far from the modern resort of Rimini).

The alarm in Rome was extreme. There were to be two Hs now in Italy, one to the north, one to the south, gnawing at the republic's vitals and ruining her economy. The best mobile troops in the southern plains were rushed north to engage Hasdrubal's invaders. Joint consuls (or generals) were chosen, to command in north and south respectively. One was Marcus Livius – a grim, moody, taciturn old soldier, with a chip on his shoulder about past injustices. Chosen as 'plebeian consul', representing the people as the law required, he was rushed to Sena.

The other chosen consul was Caius Claudius Nero, a patrician or aristocrat from one of the families of the great Claudian house. He had previously served against both Hannibal and Hasdrubal, but appeared rather young and inexperienced for so great a task as commanding the army. The leading senators fortunately noted in Nero the energy, shrewdness and spirit the situation required, and the people of Rome – who had the final say – wisely concurred. Nero went at once to Canusium, to play a cat-and-mouse game with Hannibal.

Three of Rome's six armies were in the north, but one was pinned down, restraining the disaffected Etruscans. Livius promptly welded the two disengaged armies into one, and placed them near enough to be 'in touch' with Hasdrubal's forward troops.

At this stage Hasdrubal suffered an unaccustomed stroke of ill luck. Knowing that his brother would be anxious to have detailed information of his movements and plans, and particularly as to whether he would move into Etruria or down the Adriatic coast, he prepared some letters and sent trusted messengers south with them.

But the Carthaginian messengers were intercepted by Nero's cavalry scouts and the letters were laid in Nero's hands instead of Hannibal's. They gave full particulars of Hasdrubal's camp, the strength of his forces and his intended line of march. And they revealed that the meeting place was to be South Umbria, whence together they could wheel round against Rome.

Nero saw at once how grave the crisis had

become, with the two sons of Hamilcar only 200 miles apart and ready to take the city at last.

Nero makes his move

There was a law forbidding a consul to make war or march beyond his province without written permission. Nero knew he had no time to comply. Pausing only to send a messenger to Rome to lay Hasdrubal's letters before the senate, he ordered 7,000 of his finest men, a thousand of them horsed, to hold themselves in readiness for a secret attack on one of Hannibal's garrisons, while the rest of his army maintained its watch on the Carthaginian's principal forces.

It was bluff. He had set out on a southern tack, but at nightfall he wheeled the 7,000 around, and pressed with all speed north towards Picenum, to link with Livius. He also sent horsemen ahead along his proposed line of march to tell local communities to leave stores, provisions and refreshments by the nearest roadsides. All the while he hoped he had out-bluffed the archbluffer; that Hannibal was and should remain ignorant of his feint and its true purpose.

Also, like Montgomery in World War II, Nero was a great believer in trusting his troops. When they were a league or two on the way, he halted in a natural ampitheatre and explained to the 7,000 what was in his heart, as well as what was in his mind.

Toughest march in history

'It may prove the toughest forced march in history,' Nero explained, 'but if we can do it swiftly and secretly, Rome will be saved, and you will be able to tell your grandchildren you took part in our greatest-ever victory.' And he asked them to fear nought. 'There has never been a design more seemingly audacious and more really "safe",' he concluded. Surprise would be theirs. The Carthaginians would know nothing until the Romans appeared on the battlefield.

The men responded as never before. It was to be a march unparalleled in military annals. The men caught the full spirit of their leader. Night and day they pressed on, taking meals on the march, and resting by relays in following waggons supplied by country people.

Several times, couriers passed secretly and

safely between Nero and Livius (Livius was now encamped within half-a-mile of Hasdrubal), and among the messages was one advising Nero to time his arrival so as to reach the camp by night. When the marchers reached their goal, the 7,000 were smuggled silently into the tents of their Livius-commanded comrades, each according to his rank, so that no enlargement of the camp could give the game away to the enemy.

A council of war was held at once, with Livius's officers urging rest for the weary marchers. But Nero understood the importance of striking while the bluff held. 'We must fight without undue delay,' he said, 'while both the foe here and the southern foe are ignorant of our subterfuge. Having destroyed Hasdrubal, I must be back in Apulia before Hannibal awakes from his torpor.' And the most he would agree to was one day's rest.

He need not have worried. No spy or deserter had informed Hasdrubal of Nero's arrival. Nor had his departure become known to Hannibal.

In the morning, however, there was a moment when the deceit at Metaurus was all but rumbled. As Hasdrubal rode out with the dawn patrol, he noticed there things: the armour of some of the soldiers seemed unusually dull and stained, which was strange, as Livius was known to be a spit and polish merchant; some of the horses,

Carthaginian elephants engage Roman javelin men while infantry wait to exploit the ponderous assault. But Hasdrubal lost six of his ten elephants.

too, were dirtier and more rough of coat than was normal; and the trumpets giving orders to the Roman legions sounded once oftener than usual, suggesting the arrival of a consul of greater importance than Livius.

It was the third observation that confused Hasdrubal into error. There was no actual sign of an increase in the numbers before him. The trumpet calls had to mean that there was to be a change of command ... and that was of no great consequence; he could out-think the best of them. Anyway, it was time to put his master plan into operation. This was to retreat by night to friendly country and then fight.

Hasdrubal's plan crumbles

So it was that that night, at the time of the first watch, Hasdrubal led his army silently out of their entrenchments, and northwards to the Metaurus, to place the river between himself and the Romans before his move was discovered.

But his locally-recruited guides betrayed him. They led him away from the only ford, made their escape in the dark and reported to Nero. They had been 'planted' on Nero's instructions by his advance men.

Hasdrubal's army was floundering in confusion along the steep banks, and falling in numbers into deep water. By dawn they had altogether halted in confusion, indiscipline, fatigue and frustration.

The Roman cavalry arrived on the scene at first light, to be followed shortly by the legions, marching swiftly towards instant engagement.

Hasdrubal could do little but rapidly survey the ground and get his troops into something resembling Carthaginian battle order, assembled according to the nationalities or capabilities of the men.

The armies line up

Before the whole army, he quickly lined up his ten colossal elephants, with their Ethiopian 'boy's' as a chain of mobile advanced fortresses, placed to the centre and right fore. The elephant boys were armed with a sharp spike and a mallet. If any beast threatened to run amok, it was to be killed by a blow at the junction of head and spine.

In the centre of the army proper were Hasdrubal's best warriors – Carthaginians and Phoenici-Africans. These were surrounded by half-naked Gauls, with targets, long javelins or broadswords; white-clothed Iberians; savage Ligurians; plus farther-travelled Nasamones and Lotophagi. On the wings, troops of Numidian horsemen, from all the tribes of the desert, swarmed and swanned about on unsaddled Arab horses. The van was soon occupied by Balearic slingers.

Around him, personally, Hasdrubal had a picked troop of veteran Spanish infantry, protected by helmets and shields, and armed with short cut-and-thrust swords.

Because of the rugged nature of the terrain, Hasdrubal hoped the Roman right wing would be delayed while he made some impression, with his veterans, on the Roman left.

On Nero's side, the two main divisions of legionary were drawn up ten-deep, with three feet between files (which were alternate, like men on a draught or checkers board) and three feet between the ranks. This allowed javelins to be showered on the enemy, with one line succeeding the other twice over before swords were drawn. They wore breastplates, or coats of mail, according to rank or wealth; each had brazen greaves or leg-protectors, and a brazen helmet, with a lofty, upright crest of black or scarlet feathers; each bore an oblong shield and was armed with two javelins and a short sword. The third division was held in reserve and consisted entirely of veterans. Each of these carried a spear, instead of javelins, and a cut-and-thrust sword. For the rest, the Roman army consisted of lightly-armed skirmishers, and some hundreds of highly-trained cavalrymen.

Nero commanded the right wing, as senior consul, and Livius the left, with the praetor in the centre.

As the battle opened, Livius charged the Spaniards and Africans. There was great butchery on both sides, but neither prevailed. The elephants greatly troubled the Romans, breaking their front ranks and causing their ensigns to fall back.

Meanwhile, as Hasdrubal had anticipated, Nero's right flank had to labour up a steep hill and had difficulty maintaining contact with the Gauls. Hasdrubal therefore threw even more of his forces against Livius on the left of the Roman army.

Nero's master stroke

Hasdrubal's tactics were sensible, but did not allow for Nero's genius, who, when he could not get at the Gauls, wheeled a brigade of his best men round the rear of the other two-thirds of the Carthaginian army. He then fiercely charged the flank of the Spaniards and Africans.

This charge was as successful as it was unexpected. It rolled the enemy back in sudden disorder, and, although the Spaniards and their Ligurian colleagues bravely chose to die rather than retreat, they could not stem the Roman charge with their bodies.

Instead, the way was opened to make the Gauls accessible to Nero; and he now butchered them mercilessly. Thereupon, the remaining elements of the Carthaginian second army, including its surviving elephants, fled in panic, or fell into the now-bloody waters of the river Metaurus, which was to give the great battle its name.

Hasdrubal then showed the stuff he was made of as a man. He had always schooled his men to die fighting, rather than to gratify, as captives, Roman cruelty and pride. So, having done all that a general could be expected to do in the circumstances, and knowing that there could be no hope of further resistance or of subsequent regrouping, he saw no other choice than to go down with his army.

So it was that Hasdrubal spurred his horse into the midst of a Roman cohort, where, sword in hand, he met the gory death he considered worthy of the son of Hamilcar and the brother of Hannibal.

Although Nero gained a glorious victory, his name has been almost forgotten, overshadowed by the misdeeds of the Emperor Nero who reigned 250 years later. Lord Byron, the English poet, wrote of 'the consul Nero, who made the unequalled march which deceived Hannibal and defeated Hasdrubal, thereby accomplishing an achievement almost unrivalled in military annals.

'To this victory of Nero's it might be owing that his imperial namesake reigned at all. But the infamy of the one has eclipsed the glory of the other. When the name of Nero is heard, who thinks of the consul? But such are human things.'

With the longest forced march in history, Nero deceived Hannibal for long enough to defeat Hasdrubal. The final master-stroke was taking his crack troops behind Livius.

Metaurus

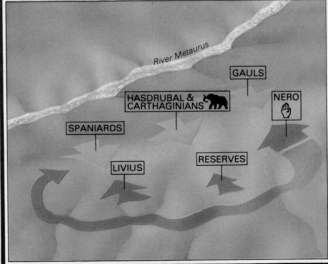

AGINCOURT

At Agincourt in France in 1415, Henry V and 5,500 troops defeated 20,000 French. The modern concept of missiles backed by infantry — the English massed archers and foot-slogging men-at-arms — was already showing its superiority over the romantic cavalry charges.

Shakespeare immortalized the classic Jack-the-Giantkiller victory of the English over the French at Agincourt with: 'We few, we happy few, we band of brothers,' in the alleged words of Henry V before the battle.

And Shakespeare could have anticipated Churchill's words about the Battle of Britain by adding: 'Never in the history of English arms were so many slaughtered by so few,' for Agincourt was also one of the world's bloodiest battles.

But there is a basic ringing difference between the two events.

Whereas Churchill was capturing an ever-lasting truth in a phrase, Shakespeare was sugaring an unpalatable pill, to give it the semblance of eternal virtue. That he succeeded is his magic rather than that of the event itself.

Henry taunts the French

The stubborn, strong-willed Henry V, like Edward III in his prime, had a natural gift of

leadership, but tended to use it as a means towards perverse ends. He was as foolish as he was brave, and was fortunate to have luck going for him a lot of the time. By all the odds, he never

Opposite Henry V was a warrior king, happy to join the fighting, but he was fortunate to win at Agincourt.

Below The English might well pray on the morning before battle for they faced a French army four times their size.

Right The long-bow and 3,000 archers gave Henry the advantage. The five-foot bow loosed a three-foot, steel-tipped arrow that could stop cavalry at 300 yards.

Overleaf In fighting at Agincourt the French forgot their own principle of victory through avoiding battle. Bogged down and with their horses floundering in the mud they died in thousands.

should have won at Agincourt. After the idiocy of his lengthy, pointless and flesh-wasting siege of Harfleur, in which he not only lost half his army as casualties, but weakened the rest with malnutrition and dysentery, he should have sailed back to England, thankful to have made one half-baked point. But this could not be, because he had dismissed his sea transports, determined to go home the hard way, to 'show' the French his contempt for their fighting qualities.

Not that the Dauphin's noble generals were any more rational. Henry's slow march, or 'Edwardian' parade, towards and across the Somme was clearly signposted. All the French had to do to destroy the tired, ragged and hungry English army was to employ against it the strategy taught them by the Constable du Guesclin. If they had kept their emotions in check, victory was theirs. The drill – by which du Guesclin had, in five years, reduced the vast English possessions in France to a slender strip between Bordeaux and Bayonne – was to *avoid* battle with the main English army, while exploiting mobility and surprise, nibbling away at the marchers to their utter dismay, always taking the line of least expectation and mostly doing so by night.

Just as other generals, in common with moneylenders, had maintained the principle of 'no advance without security', so du Guesclin's shrewd teaching had been 'no attack without surprise'.

The French mistake

Instead of following du Guesclin's ideas, the Dauphin, the French prince, was goaded by Henry's arrogance even into forgetting the lesson of Crecy, the battle 80 years earlier where Edward III's outnumbered army had beaten the French. He insisted that, with a four-to-one superiority of force, it would be shameful to use his army for anything other than a direct confrontation.

So it was that, after Henry had passed the small river of Ternoise, at Blangy in Picardy, about 40 miles from Calais, he was astonished to see the entire French army drawn up across his path, amply provisioned and heavily armed.

The scene was set for a major showdown, and the 'stars' were worthy of the scenario. Henry

had his noblest barons with him; the Dauphin – in the absence, due to madness, of his father, the king – was supported by all the princes of the blood. The underlying rivalry, jealousy, and gamesmanship had earlier been established when the Dauphin, hearing that Henry was coming to fight against him, had sent a box of tennis balls, urging the English monarch to amuse himself with them at home instead of making the 'foolish' invasion. Henry's response had been to say he would lob back gun stones instead of balls.

At Agincourt, Henry prudently drew up his army on a half-mile funnel of ground between two woods which guarded his flanks. He was wisely mindful of the fact that his situation was similar to those of Edward at Crecy, and of the Black Prince at Poitiers, and by God he was ready to show himself as fine a soldier king.

The French were foolishly posturing, their tongues rudely thrust out and their fingers to their noses, so to speak. There were over 20,000 of them against barely 5,500 on the English side.

Henry, having heard mass, rode along the lines, inspiring and jollying his weary warriors. A magnificent, instantly-recognizable extrovert figure, he had a gold crown upon his helmet, and wore a coat over his armour embroidered not only with the leopards of England, but with the lilies of France. He then dismounted and took his place among his soldiers, with the royal standard waving over him. It was October 25, Saint Crispin's Day, and the clear dawn showed the two armies already in battle positions, but contrasted ones. The French clung old-fashionedly to the idea that cavalry should dominate the field; the English put their faith in the more modern concept of massed archers and foot-slogging men-at-arms. Both sides had guns, but these were to play little part in the battle.

Overnight rain had stopped and the armies could each see the other clearly. They had plenty of opportunity for rumination, for the initial stalemate lasted for four hours.

The rout begins

At 11 a.m., Henry grew weary of the eyeball-to-eyeball business and suddenly gave the order: 'Banners Advance!' whereupon, with trumpets shrilling, the English army advanced to cries of 'St. George! St. George!'

The soggy clay on the French side had been

churned into a quagmire overnight by their thousands of horses; it was much firmer at the English end. When Henry's army was within bow-shot range of the enemy, he gave the order to halt, and the 3,000 archers thrust their palisades into the ground, forming an anti-cavalry fence behind which they could fire. In a moment there was a whooshing sound, as of water rushing, and the sky was filled with a forest of English arrows.

The French horses, already floundering in the mud, took fright the more easily as arrows fell like rain; some rushed onwards to impale themselves on the stakes, throwing their riders at the feet of the bowmen, where they were clubbed to instant death; most of the others either rolled on the ground to get the arrows out of their flesh or bolted in all directions, scattering dismounted men-at-arms and throwing their armoured riders, who remained where they fell in the mud.

The mass of the French men-at-arms ploughed on but were so crowded together as the field narrowed towards the English end that they could scarcely raise their weapons.

As dismay gave place to confusion, Henry chose exactly the right moment to advance again. His men were comparatively light and unencumbered; and being fewer in number, they had room to manoeuvre. As the English foot-soldiers began knocking down and cutting up the 'Frogs' in their hundreds, the English archers threw down their bows, took up their battleaxes and joined in with gusto. Tasting blood, they excitedly butchered their way through the first French line and straight into the second.

No prisoners to be taken

Within an hour, the piles of corpses and dying men were head high in places and Henry's unstoppable army had to climb over them to round up the remnants behind. At first these were taken as prisoners for ransom money, but at about mid-day, the king – who had fought on foot as bravely as any three men – gave the bloody order: 'No prisoners are to be taken.' He did this, it is said, because the French third line, mainly cavalry, was standing back, undecided; apparently Henry wanted to 'show' them further resistance would be madness. The fact is that the wholesale cruel slaughter went on, and even the houses to which some of the

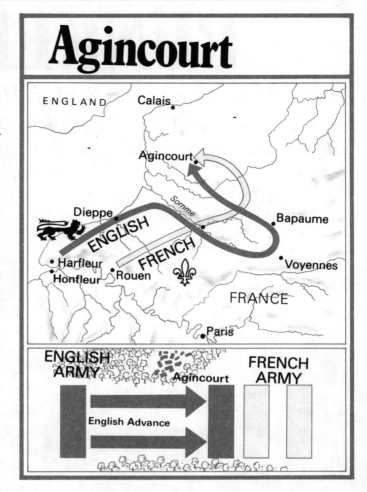

The French faced a British army weakened by lengthy forced marches. But their cavalry could not charge on the soggy ground while the British advanced within bow-shot.

wounded had been carried by their comrades were razed to the ground by fire. The third line was then rounded up, more or less intact.

When the count was taken, some said only 40 Englishmen were killed, and some said 100. Certainly, the French dead numbered over 7,000, including the highest nobles in the land, and Henry was master of at least twice as many prisoners.

Henry's army was by now too worn out to pursue its advantage. Henry returned with them to tremendous acclaim in England, and his ascendancy, as a result of the one great battle, was sufficiently assured to prevent trouble at home for the rest of his short life.

There was even a 'pop' ballad written, *The Agincourt Song*, which caught the public's imagination and helped to establish the battle in history as a great and glorious event.

BUNKER HILL

On the bloody slopes of Bunker Hill, in 1775, a thousand American farmers stood against the professional soldiers of the British Army. Their highly-successful 'guerilla' action helped kindle the American War of Independence.

Left Well dug-in, with the hill slope and cannon helping, American militia held off 3,000 regulars.

Above George Washington as a young man crowned the victory won on Bunker Hill by forcing a British evacuation of Boston.

The grisly battle of Bunker Hill, which fanned the sparks of American independence into a forest fire, came 18 months after the Boston Tea Party and nine months after the first Continental Congress.

Delegates from every province in the colonies but one had assembled in Philadelphia on 4 September, 1774, in the persons of almost all the ablest men in America; they had drawn a series of state papers, defining and defending the position of the colonies, with such caring that these were declared superior to the masterpieces of Greek or Roman statecraft; and they had drafted the splendid Declaration of Rights.

These men, although firmly against Imperial taxation, the quartering of troops, and the three recent coercion acts, made a declaration that was nonetheless far from aggressive towards the mother country.

September, 1774, was therefore the moment when inspired statesmanship could have prevented what was to become 'the most painful of all subjects for an Englishman to dwell on' – the War of Independence.

Instead, the obstinacy of the despotic King George III, the folly of his advisers and the natural pride of the freeborn sons of freeborn pioneers spoiled the moment.

The King believed the colonists could and should be beaten into obedience; they valued their freedom more than their lives; Eastern Massachusetts had risen in arms against Boston; and events moved swiftly toward the confrontation on the Charlestown peninsula through which the quarrel would pass from words to blood.

Paul Revere rides all night

The overture to the drama of Bunker Hill was in April, 1775, when patriot Paul Revere had ridden all night, as for his life, through the lanes of Massachusetts awakening villagers. His message was that they had to bar the road to Concord, near Boston, where other patriots were collecting arms and stores.

The British redcoats got no satisfaction in Concord and, on their forced withdrawal to Boston, after the unfortunate shooting of eight American minutemen at Lexington, suffered 293 casualties, killed or wounded by the shotgun blasts of hedgerow-hidden farmers.

In 1775, Britain had only 7,000 troops in all of North America, where the population numbered about 2½ million. In England and Scotland there were fewer than 10,000 able-bodied soldiers to defend Britain and to reinforce the American garrisons; and it usually took three or four months to cross the Atlantic.

The British, brainwashed by the King and his obsequious ministers, had been astounded at the turn of events, following the first Congress. Like 'German George', they did not understand the American mind, nor did they try to learn about it. They regarded the colonists as Britons across the sea, whereas the Americans had become a very different sort of people – a rebel people, ready to shake off the mass of traditions that meant so much to an Englishman.

Americans take Bunker Hill

On the morning of 17 June, 1775, General Thomas Gage, commander-in-chief of the British military force in America, an effete, supine and mild-mannered man with little grasp of the realities of the situation, sat drinking tea with his American-born wife, as he doodled with the wording of a 'progress report to the King'. He could scarcely believe the words of his adjutant who interrupted to give him news that the embattled farmers of Massachusetts had overnight occupied and fortified two hills on the Charlestown peninsula, just over the narrow Charles River from Boston. So dominant were these features that it became immediately apparent, even to the sluggish-minded Gage, that unless the redcoats could recapture the hills, holding Charlestown and maybe Boston, too, would become impossible.

The two hills, interconnected by a ridge, were Breed's Hill and Bunker Hill. They had been taken over silently by a body of about 1,000 men, under the command of William Prescott, a hero of the French war. The occupation of the Boston suburb of Charlestown was eagerly desired by the colonists, and the two hills – which should have been fortified by Gage's troops, but were not – were the vital first step strategically.

Prescott's expedition acted with such speed and carried out its work so quietly that, although the peninsula was surrounded by the British ships of war, not one watching sailor was alerted to what was going on a few hundred yards away in the dark.

Prescott more than once walked down to the shore during the night and reassured himself that his ploy was unobserved; he wrote later that he could clearly hear the British sentries going their rounds and changing guard.

Spurred into unaccustomed action, the diffident Gage set about recovering the hills. Shortly after

Right Colonel Israel Putnam, a French and Indian war veteran, ordered his men to fire at the white British gaiters and then 'at the white of their eyes'.

noon on June 17, he assembled 3,000 British troops in Boston, and they were quickly ferried across the river. At the same time, the guns of a man-of-war, *The Lively*, opened fire on the American positions, and so did a battery from Copp's Hill.

'Prescott's Thousand' continued their toil through all the pounding, apparently inspired and undismayed, encouraged by Israel Putnam, second-in-command of all Massachusetts volunteers, a courageous if illiterate farmer, and by Joseph Warren, the youthful president of the colony's Congress.

When it was found that the mass gunfire was having no effect on the colonists, Gage reluctantly decided that there was nothing for it but to have the hills stormed.

British redcoats attack

Just after three o'clock that afternoon, the 3,000 British redcoats, under the command of General William Howe, ascended Bunker Hill to make a frontal attack on the American trenches. Not a sound came from the entrenched volunteers until Howe's men were within 50 yards. Then Prescott

Bunker Hill

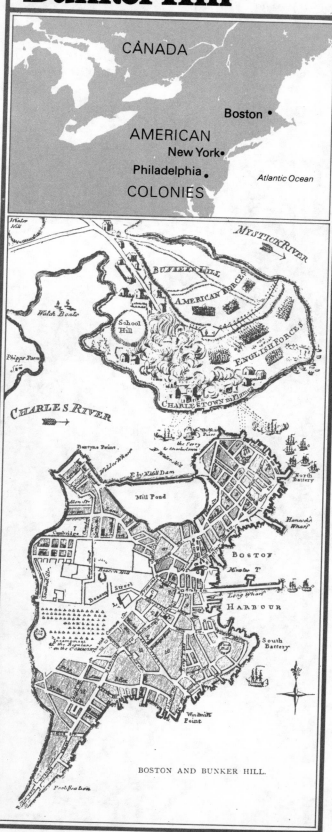

CANADA

Boston •

AMERICAN

New York •

Philadelphia •

Atlantic Ocean

COLONIES

BOSTON AND BUNKER HILL.

Left The occupation of Bunker and Breed's hills 550 yards from Charleston threatened British Boston. The British had to counter-attack.

Overleaf Cold steel prevails at the third attempt. Howe and Clinton took the hill by a flank attack with artillery support, when the Americans ran out of ammunition.

lustily gave the single crisp order: 'Fire!'

Under the terrible instant volley, the first British troops were cut to rags. Many others paused, reeled and wavered; some even ran back down Bunker Hill, all the way to the river bank.

'Do you still say the Yankees are cowards?' yelled the hill's defenders as the redcoats fell back. Americans were regarded in England as less than brave, for some odd reason, and it had been thought they would flee like sheep the moment they saw redcoats advancing under any circumstances.

Howe was a tough and single-minded general. He led his men on the attack, miraculously escaping personal injury. Twice more they were driven off before the murderous massed colonial fire. At one point, Howe found himself virtually alone on the field, and he had no choice but to withdraw, to rally and reassemble his frightened men. Every member of his personal staff had been felled, and his silk stockings were blood-spattered.

In their improvised bunkers on Bunker Hill, the men Gage had called 'the rabble of New England' were jubilant, as they awaited their third test by fire. They were as mixed a bunch – farmers, labourers and merchants – as could have been plucked from the countryside in a socio-economic sample. Maybe they were not going to be able to capture Charlestown and threaten Boston from the north, as had been the object of the exercise; maybe they were soon going to have to retreat firing, as minutemen should; but, by God, they had shown their marksmanship as well as their sheer guts. They had struck a noisy blow for freedom that day which many would hear and would follow.

This was something Gage and his fellow-sneerers had badly misjudged. The countrymen of the colonies were scant in military training, but they were probably unequalled in the world in their speed and accuracy as marksmen; the wild and wily game they tackled as individuals was much trickier to shoot than any gang of highly-disciplined redcoats.

Prescott's Thousand

As they waited for the next charge, clutching their sporting guns and old flintlocks, their powder horns by their sides, their 'uniforms' as disparate as their personalities, the insurgents' sole thoughts were how best to put a bullet in the heart of a red breast and to hell with the subtleties of battle.

There was a movement at the foot of the hill, and 'Old Put' in his command post sent a hoarse whisper echoing around the dugouts: 'Fire when you see the whites of their eyes and then retire.'

'Aye, that we will,' muttered Angus Gordon, a tough hook-nosed crofter. He raised his shotgun and spat on the ground, where his blood would soon mingle with that of a red-coated cousin from Inverness.

The embattled countrymen were all but out of bullets, and some were at the stage of improvising with nails, bolts and bits of scrap iron. But Howe did not know this, as he prepared for another assault.

Regrouped and lightened of their knapsacks, with bayonets fixed, his men again swept up Bunker Hill, with the general in the fore – six feet tall, in days when this was rare – and, although picked off by the insurgents in scores, the British succeeded in over-running the first trenches, whereupon the minutemen behind melted across the neck of the peninsula, like snow on the first day of spring.

When they had gone, the carnage on the hill was terrible to behold.

The Battle of Bunker Hill had ended as a British victory, but it was a dearly-bought one. British casualties numbered 1,054, out of 3,000 men engaged. Of Prescott's Thousand, 441 had fallen on the battlefield and others were carried away wounded.

Bunker Hill may have been a 'defeat' for the patriots, but it disproved the assumption that a farmers' army could not stand up to a regular army. And it lowered morale at Boston.

The news was carried to the second Congress in Philadelphia, where the importance of the event was at once appreciated. The Americans had shown they could and would fight for all they believed in. Three days before Bunker Hill, they had promoted Colonel George Washington to general and had made him commander-in-chief. He left at once for Boston. The War of Independence had begun.

Gage was recalled to England. Howe took charge in his stead but he was not to hold the trophy of Bunker Hill for long. He was compelled, by the superior generalship of Washington, to evacuate the hill, the peninsula, Charlestown and Boston itself in less than a year.

The second wave of British troops crosses the Charles river as Charleston burns. American reinforcements descend Bunker hill to join the men on Breed's hill.

BOSTON

CHARLES TOWN

AUSTERLITZ

The chance in 1805 to crush both Austrians and Russians forced Napoleon to fight an army bigger than his own — and stimulated his military genius to the full. Six months of brilliant strategy and confident tactics culminated in victory at Austerlitz.

French infantry advance in closely dressed ranks with muskets crooked at 'Support arm'. This tight tactical control brought as many as possible of these close-range, inaccurate weapons to bear on the enemy.

Overleaf *Napoleon's magnificent victory at Austerlitz firmly established his regime and prepared the way for further conquests.*

Austerlitz was the French Emperor's greatest battle and 1805 was Napoleon's year despite Lord Nelson's victory at Trafalgar.

After several years of uneasy peace, the curtain that had fallen on the French Revolutionary wars was now rising on a new act – the Napoleonic war, fought by Bonaparte in his new role of Emperor.

Mainly, he had built his reputation as the greatest general of his era in two ways: by compelling each foe to fight at a numerical disadvantage; and by building his own legend through self-advertisement. Always put up a bold arrogant front and you're half-way there, was his outlook.

Austerlitz was exceptional in that for once he was outnumbered in the field; for once, he risked all to win at odds of 8:7 against. But on this one occasion, the demands of the political situation overrode military calculations.

The battle was in December, 1805. Napoleon had been Emperor for 18 months. Earlier in the year he had mesmerized his enemies into a state of fumbling apprehension. In May, he had been made king of Italy in the cathedral of Milan, with the iron crown of the Lombard Kings; at the same time he had 'acquired' the republic of Genoa. He tore up treaties and contemptuously tramped on small states. Having neutralized Prussia, he felt ready by July to invade Britain. Only the Royal Navy stood in his way, and he had plans to dispose of that. Spain and the five German states were subservient allies. His appetite for aggrandizement seemed insatiable.

Like Hitler, his ambitions would drown through his ultimate inability to cross the English Channel. Like Hitler, he underrated the British and did not read the signs correctly. When the news of Trafalgar would reach dictator Napoleon, on the eve of Austerlitz, he was to regard it as an accute irritant rather than the writing on the wall; for his preoccupations had become European.

Napoleon went out among his soldiers on the morning before battle and their enthusiastic welcome heralded a day of triumph.

He had failed in only one other way in 1805, and that was in his efforts to separate the Austrians from the Russians on the principle he lived by, which stated: 'Divide, in order to subsist; concentrate, in order to fight.' Now his chance was coming to crush both in one blow, so the superior odds against him had to be faced. It was far too good a chance to miss.

Napoleon takes his chance

On August 28, the French army of about 200,000 which had been lined up, with flat-bottomed landing craft, to invade England from Boulogne, was given the order 'About turn!' and was force-marched towards the Rhine. It was characteristic Napoleonic opportunism.

He calculated that the Austrians would send an army into Bavaria to block the Black Forest exits, and he planned a wide manoeuvred march around their northern flank, across the Danube (which he reached in six weeks) and on to the Lech. He explained to his troops in advance this intended strategic barrage across the Austrians' rear.

It worked brilliantly, and this closing down of the rear led to the almost bloodless surrender of the outnumbered Austrians, under their 'paper tiger', General Mack, at Ulm, and the taking of 30,000 prisoners.

But Ulm had not finally crushed the Austrians, the more so as they knew the Russians were on the march to save them, and other Austrian armies were due to return from Italy and the Tyrol.

One of Napoleon's worries was that in crossing Austria he had gathered thousands of pressed soldiers and the size of his army was threatening to become inconvenient. The space between the Danube and the mountains to the south-west was

French cannon bombard the helpless 5,000 Austro-Russian troops trapped on the marshes below Platzen. Two hundred men and 25 guns drowned in icy water.

too cramped for any local indirect approach and there was not time for an Ulm-like wide-ranging manoeuvre.

And already the Russians were drawn up upon the Inn to shield the Austrians until their 'foreign' armies could have time to join them, from the south, through Carinthia.

The indirect approach

Napoleon's answer was to use a series of variations on the ancient theme of the indirect approach—the grand strategy which, as used in the overthrow of Persia by Alexander, and Carthage

Left Napoleon's energy was his great asset. His strategic speed and surprise at Austerlitz was unsurpassed.

Below One of the 7,000 French cavalry at the battle. They successfully fought off 15,000 enemy horsemen.

by Scipio, had given birth to the Macedonian and Roman empires. This was the moment for him firmly to establish his European empire by doing likewise.

First, by subtly forcing the Russians to move eastwards he was able to separate them from the Austrian army returning from its successes in Italy. He advanced directly east towards Vienna, while sending a corps under Mortier along the north bank of the Danube. This forced the Russian general, Kutosov, his communications threatened, to fall back northeastwards to Krems.

French general Joachim Murat was then sent dashing across Kutosov's new flank towards Vienna, which he took without a struggle on November 13. Thence, Murat moved northwards on Hollabrunn, to menace the Russian army's left rear, and they were driven into another scrambled retreat north-east, almost to their own frontier, at Olmutz, where they were able to draw reinforcements; but they had been forced by Napoleon to abandon their original role of protecting Austria until the Italian-based army arrived.

Time was now of the essence for Napoleon, because Prussia had turned-coat and seemed likely to bring an army of 180,000 to the help of the allies before long. Also, his general position remained less than secure; his corps were scattered in a gigantic semi-circle, from Pressburg almost to Brunn, with winter under way.

Napoleon therefore pursued the indirect approach he had been following by feigning weakness and retreat. This tempted the two Russian armies, as he had hoped, into taking the offensive.

He concentrated a mere 50,000 of his troops at Brunn, against the enemy's 80,000, and pushed out isolated detachments towards Olmutz. He also sent emissaries to plead for peace talks, and, when the enemy swallowed this poisoned bait, he recoiled before them to a position he had carefully pre-studied near Austerlitz, which could form a natural snare for his too-unwary foes.

Czar and Emperor

The allies were led, titularly, by two autocratic emperors—the young Czar Alexander of Russia (a German by descent and by marriage) and the Emperor Francis II of Austria. Their plan—put to them by the Austrian general Weirother, a favourite of the Czar—was to turn the right wing of the French army and so cut off their connections with Vienna. Napoleon, again reading their ponderous minds, had encouraged their design by abandoning the Platzenberg, a move which persuaded them he still intended to retreat, with his meagre force of 50,000. The allies rejoiced, believing that, for once, they had had the Corsican pig on the run, because of their superior numbers, and they foolishly ignored the lesson—demonstrated for a decade—that French troops under Napoleon could be made to march two miles to anybody else's one.

Ensnared, although they did not know it, the two emperors and their staff officers took over Austerlitz castle at the end of November and on December 1 established their armies on the nearby defensible plateau of Platzen—where their centre could be weakened with impunity—exactly as the cunning Corsican had wanted.

Meanwhile, in the 60 hours before the battle, Napoleon brought up a division at the trot, from Pressburg, 70 miles to the south, and a corps from Iglau, 50 miles to the east—all unknown to the allies—to the point that he had nearly 70,000 men to the allies' 80,000. This he deemed just

about enough for his purposes, his tactics could offset his rare deficiency in numbers.

Napoleon celebrates

So confident was Napoleon on the morning of December 2 that he went out to visit the soldiers at the bivouacs, and they were no less enthusiastic. Someone had recalled that December 2 was the anniversary of the emperor's coronation and spontaneously the troops gathered up the straw upon which they had been sleeping, made it into bundles, and lit these at the end of poles, in celebration of the event.

This sudden pre-dawn blaze was taken on the allied side to be a further indication of the impending flight of the French forces. Before the

A chasseur à cheval from one of 24 regiments. These light horse were used in pursuit and scouting, especially to screen Murat's movements before Austerlitz.

Austerlitz

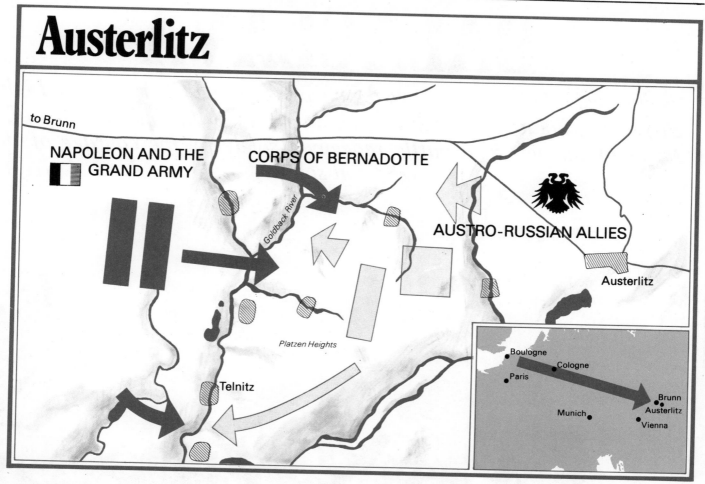

early bitterly-cold morning mists had lifted, 30,000 of the Austro-Russian troops sought to hasten this retreat by hurling themselves against the French right, driving it from the village of Telnitz and across the Goldbach. This was as Napoleon had predicted to his soldiers. He encouraged the allies thus to extend their left against his retreating right, until they found themselves stretched over a long arc, with their possession of the outside lines a handicap.

This was the moment Napoleon was waiting for; he swung round his centre against the weakened 'joint'; storming the heights of the Platzenberg, a French corps held off all attempts by the Russian horse and foot to retake this key position.

The allied armies were falling apart at the centre, where Napoleon was personally leading the infantry of the guard, and the corps of Bernadotte; and the extended right wing was not only unable to help, but failed to extricate itself from a trap set for it, and was swept into frozen marshes, where hundreds fell through the ice and drowned as French cannon balls landed at their sides.

By the close of the winter day, the two allied

Napoleon marched his army half-way across Europe then tempted 85,000 Austro-Russians into trying to crush him against the river Goldback. Reinforced, he split them on the Platzen Heights.

emperors had abandoned the bloody battlefield in despair. Behind them, they could hear French cries of victory as the cavalry pursued the vanquished; around them were the groans of the wounded and the imprecations of the fugitives.

Austerlitz had been taken over by the conquerors. The emperors sought safety in the imperial castle of Halitsch, and sent Prince John of Lichtenstein to ask from Napoleon an armistice and an interview.

Austerlitz shattered the Czar's confidence, and forced Francis to abandon the coalition.

Napoleon again summoned his troops the next day and said: 'Soldiers, I am satisfied with you . . . In France, my people will see you again with joy, and it will suffice for you to say: "I was at the battle of Austerlitz," to receive the reply: "There indeed is a hero!" '

BALACLAVA

'Someone had blundered' says the poem about the Charge of the Light Brigade at Balaclava in the Crimea in 1854. It was only the last of a series of idiocies in a battle redeemed solely by the courage of the common soldier.

Idiotic diplomacy begat the Crimean war. Massive inefficiency characterized its conduct. It was a lustful, useless war, which Britain, France and Russia drifted into, and which scarcely anyone wanted. Even when the drift had become irreversible, the generals had difficulty in deciding where or how it should be fought. And when the Crimea had been chosen, because Napoleon III feared he might be as unlucky as his uncle if he went anywhere near continental Russia, what should have been a short sharp victory became instead a tragic series of bungled nonsenses in a year of misery for all concerned.

Victory to the soldiers

Yet the common British soldier – frozen, undernourished, badly clothed and frequently flogged – fought with such bravery at Balaclava, for no cause other than that of pride, that the pointless and inconclusive battle is still talked of as a great and glorious victory.

He did this led by old and useless generals; by pink young men who had bought their commissions.

The allied armies had landed in the Crimea, during September 14 to 16, 1854, to begin the war which had been six months declared.

The Czar's naval forces had declined battle with the British and French fleets in the Black Sea, and had retired to Sebastopol harbour, so that the Crimean operations were almost exclusively military.

The British were led by General Lord Raglan,

The 17th Lancers lead the 'Gallant Six Hundred' into the 'Valley of Death'. Lord Cardigan, on the left, in his 11th Hussars uniform heads the Light Brigade.

and the French by Marshal Leroy de St-Arnaud. Raglan was brave but mediocre and stupid as well as old; St-Arnaud was dying. They quarrelled constantly, not least because Raglan, in his dotage, kept referring to the French as 'the enemy'. This was the more odd because he had previously never even commanded a battalion in the field, having been behind a desk for 40 years and more.

Somehow, an equally-muddled Russian army was defeated at the Alma on September 20. St-Arnaud promptly died, to be replaced by the equally-uninspired General F. C. Canrobert. The allies could and should have followed through promptly. They could have entered Sebastopol from the north; instead, after characteristic arguments and indecisions, they eventually marched to the south, and camped around the harbour of Balaclava, the ancient Portus Symbolon.

This allowed the Russians, under General Todleben, to throw up defensive works at Sebastopol – an immensely strong fortress – and these would hold the allies at bay for another 12 months; it would also enable the Russians to build up from 40,000 to 100,000 men. Nor were the allies equipped for a siege of *any* length.

Disease and frost

In the bitterly cold and desolate wastes around the insanitary allied tents and trenches, disease and vermin caused almost incredible conditions. Lice, bugs and fleas were everywhere; scurvy, cholera and dysentery claimed hundreds of lives. Britain had been at peace for 40 years, and everyone had forgotten how to plan a war. While the troops shivered and starved at Balaclava, stores of unreachable clothing and food were piling up in the wrong ports; when a shipload of boots arrived at the proper port, they were found to be all for the left foot. Terrible storms wrecked other supply vessels. The same storms blew away the Balaclava tents, so that the troops had to sleep on wet straw in the snow and frost, and this in cold so dreadful that rifle barrels froze to men's hands and tore away the skin when removed. In the crowded hospitals (before the arrival of Florence Nightingale and her 38 nurses after the battle) the dirt, horror and indifference were dreadful.

Such was the scene in Balaclava on the eve of the battle.

Because it was 39 peacetime years since

Waterloo, the army was also rusty and unprofessional in its officer class. The youngest of all possible generals, from whom Raglan was chosen, were in their sixties.

The way to the top

Lord Cardigan had achieved command of the Light Brigade of Cavalry, without ever seeing a shot fired in anger, by a fairly typical route. He had bought his way to the top of the 15th Hussars for £30,000, and had lost his command after a scandal; he had then paid £40,000 for the top rank in the 11th Light Dragoons, and had, this time survived until promotion had to be given him. General Scarlett, his opposite number with the Heavy Brigade, was equally ignorant, languid and 'green'.

The commander of the Cavalry Division, Lord Lucan, Cardigan's brother-in-law, was probably even more vapid than the other two. Like 'Major Major Major Major' in *Catch 22*, Lord Lucan (known to the troops as Look-on) was the ultimate in mediocrity.

Nor were cavalry activities in the campaign helped by a bitter feud Lucan and Cardigan had been engaged in since childhood, which both considered more pressing, even on the battlefield, than any face-to-face with the Russians. Indeed, Lord Wolseley (when commander-in-chief) would say of these two: 'If they had been private soldiers, no colonel would be stupid enough to promote them to the rank of corporal!' And a French general said of all three cavalry officers: 'They were brave because they were too dim to discern an alternative.'

Cavalry has its day

Balaclava is remembered for its horses as much as for its men. In 1874, cavalry were still a large part of the cult of the conqueror, horse-worship having long been a part of the British way of life. The theory was that the man on the horse was not only more powerful and bigger than the infantryman, but he was faster and more robust. He was also a superior being, to be horse-borne

In close-order British infantry are drilled with iron discipline. First and 4th Divisions marched in such a manner and failed to fire a shot in the battle.

at all, and it is worthy of note that, to this day, cavalry regiments take precedence over infantry-men of the British Army

The unpalatable truth, generally ignored, is that, in point of military history, cavalry has had a very up and down record as against infantry. Nothing can kill the cult and the 'glamorized' legend of British 'warhorses' and their associa-tion with the aristocracy, as at Balaclava. It is no chance that the Queen takes the salute, at the Trooping the Colour parade, on horseback (rather than standing by the Mausoleum, like a Russian military leader), and the British still refuse to eat horsemeat, for no coherent reasons.

The Russians had about 50,000 troops avail-able for the attack on Balaclava, and the allies had 66,000, but only a few thousand British and Russian mounted troops, and some guns were involved in the curiously unreal battle, during the last great war to be fought in scarlet and gold, according to the military equivalent of the Queensberry Rules of the Ring. Nor were the French and Turks involved to blur the pattern.

Lord Raglan's headquarters were on the Sapoune Ridge, some five miles out from Balaclava, and about 25,000 of his besieging troops were around him. Balaclava itself was but lightly guarded and the British could have been cut off from their supplies at almost any time by any force less dim than the Russians.

File to your lines

In the pre-dawn half-light, on October 24, the anniversary of Agincourt, half the Russian army (consisting of 20,000 infantry, 3,000 cavalry, and 78 guns) was seen to be advancing through the eastern approaches towards the North Valley which faced the British. The Cavalry Division, which had been 'standing to horses', was ordered to 'file to your lines' and was drawn up at the other end of the valley, just outside Russian gun range, the Light Brigade to the left, the Heavy to the right, directly under Raglan's 'eyrie', whence he proposed to watch the battle through his spy-glass.

A British horse battery of two howitzers and four six-pounders unlimbered near the Causeway to the right of the valley, between the second and third redoubt. Another battery of guns was established to the north of the Causeway.

Cardigan, who was still asleep in his private

Above Lord Raglan, the British commander at Balaclava who lost his right arm at Waterloo, still sometimes thought he was fighting the French.

Right Two squadrons of the Royal Scots Greys (2nd Dragoons) lead the charge of the Heavy Brigade.

yacht in the bay, was roused; various wives were sent for so that they could 'enjoy' the sight of the battle from Raglan's hill-top hq, just as a Russian cannonade of some power opened the proceedings. A small party of Turks in the most forward redoubt on Canrobert's Hill, hopelessly outgunned and seeing no hope of relief from the British, fell back, as did their compatriots on the Causeway Heights, from the second of the six redoubts. These latter were pursued by Cossack cavalry and many were cut to pieces without mercy.

Too many Russians

Seeing the port of Balaclava threatened, the British sent troops from the northern flank to reinforce the small garrison; this exposed the third (strategically most important) redoubt in the heart of the North Valley. Its Turkish occupants fled screaming 'Too many Russians', as did those of the fourth redoubt at the other end of the valley, in front of the cavalry division. The British NCOs who had led them remained long enough to spike the guns of the second, third and fourth redoubts. All this negative

activity had taken up the first hour of the battle, and some time had been gained to get most of the British officers to the scene. By the laws of war (British version) nothing positive could happen in the game until the captains of the teams were present.

Raglan's first order, sent at some leisure by foot from his almost inaccessible post, was to the cavalry, and it was for them to retreat behind the 'safe' sixth redoubt, still nearer to him.

At this point, the Russians, with great superiority of numbers, could have overwhelmed the

The 1st Division took a roundabout route to the plain, to avoid any confrontation with the Russians, and was astonished, when on the Sapoune heights, to see an immense body of Cossacks, in close formation, accompanied by artillery and followed by infantry, moving up the North Valley. In due course, Raglan, with the

The 17th Lancers have reached the 12 Russian guns, but Cossacks are counter-charging. Blunt sabres and lances reduced losses in such melees.

British, but they were ditherers, too, and they did nothing. A lull of some hours descended on the battlefield, while Raglan gave the order for a frugal breakfast for the troops, to be washed down with a welcome tot of rum, and called in two reserve divisions, the 1st and 4th, in support; but the 4th was delayed because its commander, Sir George Cathcart, refused to hurry his breakfast and sat in his tent drinking coffee for 40 minutes after the order had reached him. It would have been funny had it not been so tragic.

over-cautious Canrobert beside him, saw this, too, with panic in his heart.

Heavy Brigade in action

Thinking the Russians were headed direct for Balaclava, by-passing him, Raglan ordered eight squadrons of the Heavy Brigade to attack the Russians, who were now in sight, over the causeway ridge. The 'Heavies' were at a tactical disadvantage, on lower ground; they were strung out in two lines; and they were led by a courageous but short-sighted inexperienced dolt, Scarlett. They were also about 300 strong against the Russian's 2,000 or more horses, now not more than half a mile away.

Stupidly ignoring the Russians' rapid approach, Scarlett and his officers placed themselves in front of their troopers, their backs to the enemy, put out markers, and unhurriedly dressed them by the right, as they had learned to do on the parade grounds of Hounslow and Phoenix Park in Britain. Nor was the ritual hurried when the trumpeter, on Lucan's order, sounded the charge.

Again the Russians had the chance of a lifetime. Again they allowed themselves to be astounded to see Scarlett, his aide-de-camp, his trumpeter and his orderly charging towards them at full tilt, while the squadrons behind them got slowly into movement, through the walk, the trot and the gallop, as was the correct drill.

A Russian retreat

The fearless four arrived at the Russian fore a full 60 yards ahead of the rest and somehow slashed their way through the massed ranks. The arrival of the British squadrons was also allowed to happen without real resistance, other than a few wild carbine shots, and for minutes the disorganized, bewildered Russians waited for an

The Thin Red Line of the 93rd Argyll and Sutherland Highlanders stopped the Russians from reaching the port of Balaclava.

bamboozled by the British pantomime. They halted in tight formation, about 400 yards away from Scarlett's backside, staring blankly, unbelievingly to their front. And they watched for long minutes while Scarlett completed the drill, gave 'Eyes front!' and turned to face them.

They were still stationary when the commander of the Heavy Brigade suddenly ordered the 'Charge'. He did this in such a way that only those nearest to him heard it at first, with the result that the Russians were still further order that was never given. Their general was speechless, apparently affronted. The Scots Greys and the Inniskillings cut and hacked their way into the enemy, fighting like heroes, soon to be followed by several squadrons of Dragoons. Too late the Russian general realized the mistake he had made in receiving the charge standing still, instead of at the counter-charge, and he led the retreat to safety behind the lines of the sheltering guns along the Causeway.

The English had muddled through once again.

All this while, the Light Brigade had stood to one side, 500 yards away, motionless. It would not have been 'cricket' for them to interfere, and, in any event, Lord Cardigan had not yet arrived from his yacht. Even when the Russians fled and

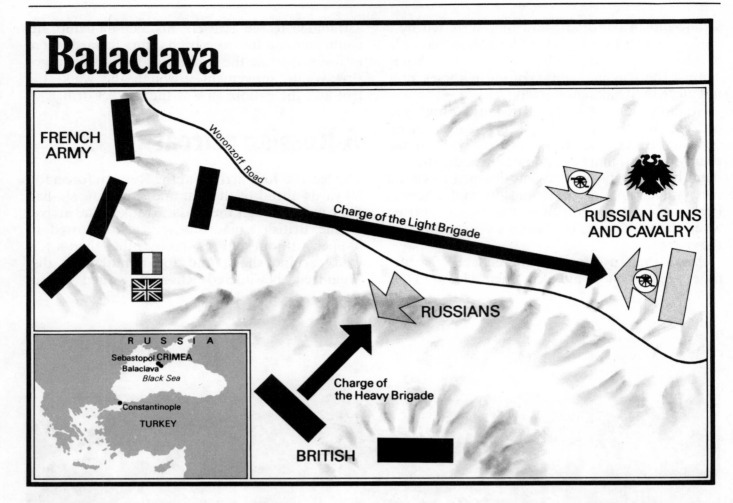

Balaclava

FRENCH ARMY

Woronzoff Road

Charge of the Light Brigade

RUSSIAN GUNS AND CAVALRY

RUSSIANS

Charge of the Heavy Brigade

R U S S I A

Sebastopol CRIMEA
Balaclava
Black Sea

Constantinople
TURKEY

BRITISH

positive action, in the form of pursuit, was obviously called for, neither Lucan nor Cardigan *did* anything, and Scarlett chose to re-muster his squadrons.

In due course, however, the Light Brigade was to have its moment of bloody pantomime, and, through it, Balaclava was to be immortalized in Alfred Lord Tennyson's epic poem of the Charge.

Charge of the Light Brigade

Lord Raglan and his party had been seated on rocks, like playgoers in the circle, watching the battle. He now decided it was time to bring the infantry into play, as well as the Light Brigade into the action. He sent a characteristically unclear order down the hill. It got thoroughly garbled. Lord Lucan interpreted it as an order for his remaining cavalry brigade to charge down the valley (actually Raglan had wanted him to recapture the redoubts on the heights). Cardigan protested that it was suicidal so to proceed. But

The Light Brigade were supposed to exploit the success of the 'Heavies' by recapturing the Causeway Heights but instead advanced straight down North Valley – the 'Valley of Death'.

he nevertheless went through all the drills and led the charge across the mile and a half of frozen soil towards the Russian batteries straight ahead, and through the flanking cross-fire of other guns and riflemen, only to have to double back again through the mayhem of the plain.

In half an hour, nearly 500 of the 673 officers and troopers had been killed, wounded, or dis-horsed, in the inferno of fire. Cardigan was spared to walk his horse round the rear, across the valley to safety, partly because the Russian Prince Radzivil had recognized him as a society acquaintance, as he rode between the guns, and had ordered that he should be captured rather than killed. He had done enough, he felt. A hot bath was called for. He was apparently indifferent to the shambles he had left behind. But first he wrapped himself in a blanket and slept exhausted on the ground near the Brigade camp – overcome by his exertions.

Bravery was all; intelligence, knowledge and organization were of no account.

The operations were then suspended. The wretched Russians, with apparently no more heart for the fight, were allowed to hold on to the three redoubts. And the siege, interrupted only by the Battle of Inkerman, continued for the best part of a year.

Balaclava was a victory *manqué*. Nor was the Crimean War a success. Certainly, as far as political objectives were concerned, it accomplished virtually nothing.

The casualties were terrible to contemplate, and 88 per cent of the 20,000 British victims of the war fell to disease and deprivation.

The 'rag trade' probably benefited most from the lah-de-dah fashions of the officers concerned. The battle and the campaign begat the Raglan coat sleeve, the Cardigan and the Balaclava helmet.

Overleaf The Light Brigade had 195 mounted survivors, leaving 113 dead and 134 wounded with 231 unhorsed men. But the rigours of camp **below**, the climate and lack of medical care killed far more.

SECOND BULL RUN

The bonfire of captured stores lit by 'Stonewall' Jackson's Confederate troops after defeating the Northerners at Bull Run in 1862 could be seen in Washington, capital of the North. It was the high spot for the South during the American Civil War.

Second Bull Run

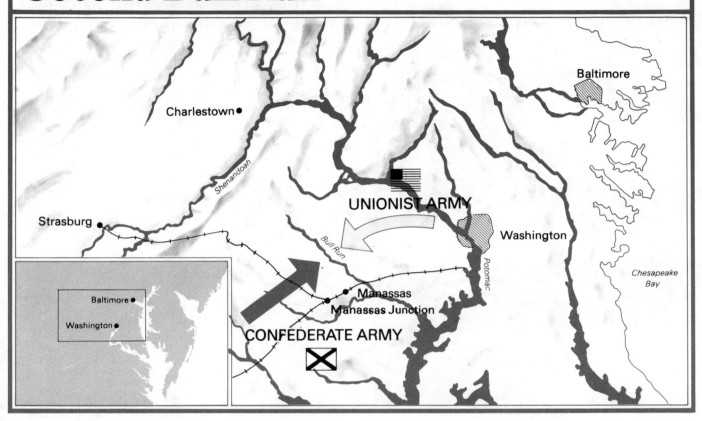

Charlestown

Baltimore

Shenandoah

UNIONIST ARMY

Strasburg

Bull Run

Washington

Potomac

Chesapeake Bay

Manassas
Manassas Junction

CONFEDERATE ARMY

Baltimore

Washington

There are many shades between black and white in any argument, but the clash between the northern and the southern states in America, in the 1860s, clearly sprang from the question of slavery, whatever nuances there may have been. Largely condemned in the relatively progressive and democratic North, slavery was the basis of a distinctive aristocratic society in the South.

The actual Civil War which stemmed from this was fought, when Abraham Lincoln was made President, to decide whether the South had the right to secede from the Union and pursue its own ways in a separate republic, the Confederate States, under its own man, Jefferson Davis.

The high-water mark

The Second Battle of Bull Run, sometimes called Second Manassas, in August 1862, was a high-water mark for the Confederates. It was also the beginning of a dreary record of defeat for the Union cause in Virginia, in which the North's commanders were outwitted and outfought by

Left '*Stonewall' Jackson whose daring raid on Manassass Junction 'set up' a second Southern victory at Bull Run.*

Above A new Union army formed to threaten the Southern capital found itself defeated 23 miles from its own.*

brave bands of Confederates, under General Robert E. Lee's restlessly-ambitious crop of lieutenants: Longstreet, the Hills, Ewell, Stuart, and the astonishing Thomas 'Stonewall' Jackson.

The First Battle of Bull Run had been in July 1861, when 20,000 Union men, under General McDowell, had been humiliated into a panic-stricken rout, to the point that the fall of the capital became a sudden frightening possibility. After the battle, the frightened northerners had built up a well-equipped army of 150,000 men, and had decided on an 'Anaconda' strategy for 1862 which would hinge on Northern pincer offensives in both the west and east, following the blockade of the entire Southern coast.

Politics, however, smothered the good intentions of the North's strategists, and fumbling

SECOND BULL RUN

Left Supplies for the campaign of 1862 at Yorktown which had been captured by Federal troops.

Below Manassass junction after Jackson's visit on August 27th. The rail bridge was broken and anything that could not be carried off was burnt that night.

Overleaf Sigel's German Union corps furiously assaults Jackson on the first day of Second Bull Run.

defence rather than driving attack was becoming the order of the day by mid-1862. Their dictatorial commander-in-chief, young George B. 'Little Napoleon' McClellan had his wings clipped, when Congress reduced him in rank to commander of the Army of the Potomac. He was ordered to remain on the Virginia Peninsula and defend Washington.

Lincoln called John Pope from the west to command a new army to march from Washington to Richmond. McClellan was then ordered to leave the Peninsula and pull back to Washington. The intention was that he should unite with Pope and resume the drive on the Confederate capital. General Lee guessed what was afoot. His response was to deal first with Pope. On August 9, Stonewall Jackson intercepted a detachment of Pope's army at Cedar Mountain and routed it. There followed a series of manoeuvres which forced Pope's main forces to retreat to the apparent

security of the north side of the Rappahannock River, where he proposed to wait until McClellan's troops reinforced him.

Lee's counter-plan was brilliant, if risky. Against all text-book rules, he divided his army. One half, under 'Stonewall' Jackson, was sent hot-foot to the north-west, around Pope's flank, while the other half, under General James Longstreet, was kept facing Pope to hold his attention. and camouflage the diversion.

Stonewall Jackson

Jackson's fast-moving infantry, making record time, swung off behind Bull Run mountains –

which he knew well. He had got his heroic name in the first battle of Bull Run, when General Bee had said: 'Look at Jackson! There he stands, like a stone wall.'

Thence he speeded east through Thoroughfare Gap, whence he was able to surprise and overwhelm the Unionists' supply base at Manassas junction, in Pope's rear. This caused the Union army to turn away defensively from Longstreet, which, in turn, gave Lee and Longstreet the chance to slip away to join Jackson east of the mountains. It was bluff, counter-bluff, and it succeeded brilliantly.

John Pope now became thoroughly confused. He had a stubborn energetic courage, but he was somewhat slow-thinking, and Lee had always been able to read his intentions. Pope chased his mobile army 'around the houses', looking for Jackson, who had, in truth, moved his 25,000 men out from Manassas as swiftly as he had pounced. And he had, unknown to Pope's scouts, taken up concealed positions in the hills and in the natural cover of the wooded thickets of the winding stream of the familiar battlefield at Bull Run. So well hidden were the Confederates that Pope's infantrymen thoroughly exhausted themselves

Left *Federal General John Pope who boasted that his HQ was 'in the saddle'. Lee retorted 'headquarters on his hindquarters!'*

Below *A Union battery of artillery is about to fire. The men are ramming home the powder and shot.*

and his cavalry got in a lather, whipping from hill to hill without catching sight of even one southerner.

When the Northern army finally made contact with the Southern on the slopes of Bull Run on August 29, it was more by good luck than judgement. Pope was by now like an enraged bull. He forced his tired, partly-trained militia – Irishmen from New York and Boston; Germans from St. Louis; Pennsylvanian farm boys clutching flintlocks; and some well-schooled career soldiers – to battle up the hill in headlong assault.

In the skirmishing that followed, the North did so well that the Southerners held their entrenched ground with great difficulty and some considerable loss, before apparently retreating.

In fact, as darkness fell, Jackson had chosen deliberately to withdraw to a second line of defence. And the foolish Pope misread the situation to the point that he sent a messenger galloping off to Washington, 23 miles away, with a dispatch which read: 'Enemy in full retreat; am preparing to pursue and harry.'

The Confederates attack

In the morning, he woke up with egg on his face. Jackson's losses had been bearable. He had regrouped and was holding the same hill just as strongly, a bit higher up. Lee and Longstreet had arrived on the scene. They nibbled at Pope's flank,

and at the same moment Stonewall Jackson switched from defence to attack.

His men were devoted to him; he was probably better loved than any general of the period. A West Point man, he was a general at the age of only 38. He had, above all things, the sort of honest, open style of command that ensured absolute loyalty.

Nor did any Confederate officer or soldier fail him at this important moment of the war. He had trained them well in small arms – having been a professor at Lexington Military Institution just before the war – and he led his cumbersome army personally, without fear or hesitation. Stonewall was steady as a rock in the heart of the battle.

Each opposing force tried to turn his opponent's left flank, and for a time North and South were locked in hand-to-hand skirmishing, men on both sides waving flags when not in contact, and each side trying to out-shout the other in its version of a popular song of the day, 'Flag of the Free'. Irish immigrants on opposing sides shouted Gaelic expletives at each other as they hacked away with a will. 'It was very unreal,' said an eye-witness, 'this fighting between brothers, cousins and ex business friends. The Northerners seemed to have less heart in the proceedings than the men of the South, but that was probably because of the superiority of the South's leadership.'

Jackson breaks through

Although in the last hours of the battle, some of McClellan's divisions succeeded in joining up with Pope's army, Jackson's frontal attack finally broke through and reduced the Union army to disorder. Crushed and dispirited, it fled to the north of Bull Run and all the way back to Washington.

It was a remarkable Confederate victory. General Pope had lost the day, his reputation as the scourge of the west, his nerve and his prospects. He had also lost some 16,000 of his army – dead, wounded and prisoners – plus many horses and all his artillery.

Confederate losses were serious but less heavy. Jackson's men were in great good spirits. They went on to deal the final humiliation of Pope's defeat when they captured intact all the Union army's stores and the general's headquarters, in a brilliant post-battle move, schemed by Stonewall Jackson. The stores, filling a train of cars two miles long, were burned after the Confederates had taken all the plunder they could carry . . . and the light of the extravagant bonfire could be clearly seen at the White House in Washington.

A Union gun crew stand by their field-gun. It is probably a 3-inch Parrott rifled muzzle-loader which fired a ten pound smooth metal banded shell spun by the rifling. A light, accurate gun it had a range of 1,900 yards. The man on the right is about to fire the piece by a long lanyard that enables him to stand away from the gun's recoil. On the right of the breach is the Parrott's pendulum sight.

SOMME

Slaughter on a scale never seen before or since was the trade-mark of the offensive on the Somme in France of 1916 as the British, under General Haig, and French tried to drive the Germans back by sheer weight of numbers — and paid the price.

Below Two British machine-gunners, wearing gas helmets, fire at a German communication trench. The fire-power of the machine-gun took a fearsome toll of any infantry advance – this Vickers .303-inch Mark I fired about 500 rounds a minute.

Right Five miles was the gain from 140 days of fighting through the blood-soaked mud of the Somme – five miles and honours for the generals.

Somme

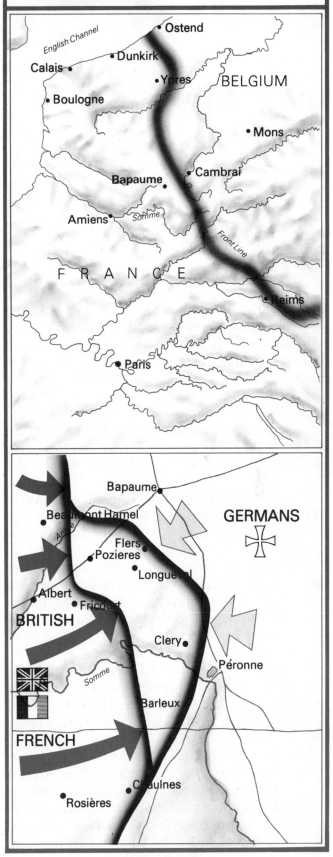

The battle of the Somme should have sickened mankind of warfare forever. The sheer bestiality of deadlocked trench fighting on this scale is almost unimaginable: slime, blood, rats, thirst, filth, gas, metal showers, fear of death, despair and madness . . . these things are so beyond the normal as to demand revolt. And yet, on the Somme during 1916, men on both sides went on enduring them for months. There were, indeed, mutinies in the French army, but not in the British.

The period between July 1, 1916, and April, 1917, which embraced the Somme offensive and the retreat which followed, was the bloodiest of the whole bloody war.

The Western Front, where the Somme river lay, was the critical front, and everyone on both sides of it knew, by the end of June, 1916, that it was about to be put to the test. At this moment, the German line stretched in sickle-shape from Switzerland to the shores of Belgium.

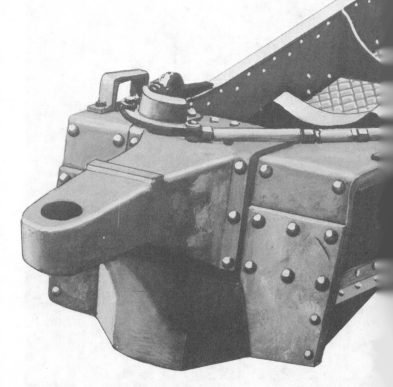

The sector of the line that seemed to offer the best outcome to successful attack was that covering Ypres and Compiegne. Here the lines of communications of the German army in France and Belgium could be cut.

The British held about 90 miles of the front, from above Ypres to the Somme. The French were in an adjacent sector, to the south. Amiens, the city on the Somme, the spider in the centre of a web of communications stretching all over Normandy, was to be the base from which the

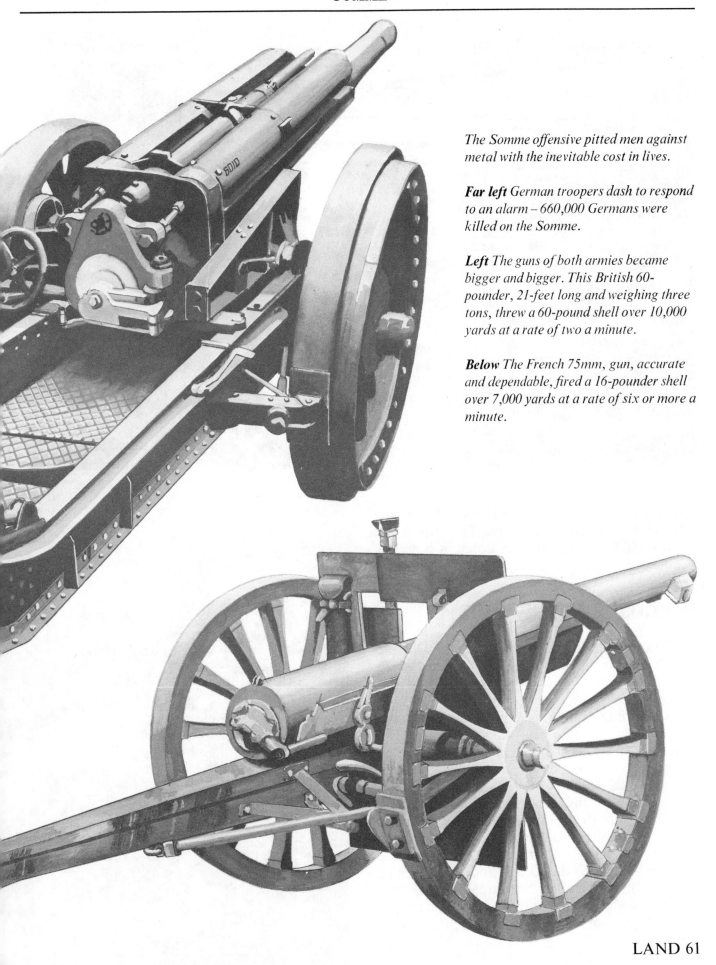

The Somme offensive pitted men against metal with the inevitable cost in lives.

Far left German troopers dash to respond to an alarm – 660,000 Germans were killed on the Somme.

Left The guns of both armies became bigger and bigger. This British 60-pounder, 21-feet long and weighing three tons, threw a 60-pound shell over 10,000 yards at a rate of two a minute.

Below The French 75mm, gun, accurate and dependable, fired a 16-pounder shell over 7,000 yards at a rate of six or more a minute.

Allies would strike.

The Germans were massed beyond the low hills which sheltered the plains. This meant the British had to attack up steep slopes in generally hostile country.

Bombs, gas and guns

The most ambitious campaign in which the British had ever been engaged opened with several days of bombardment, by artillery and from the air. Poison gas was dropped at least 40 times. Aerial photographs were taken of the German lines on the north bank of the river. The light field guns had a special task: to destroy the miles of woven barbed wire, devised as an initial obstacle to advancing troops.

The heavy guns concentrated on concrete redoubts with steel emplacements for machine guns. Trench mortars of all sizes accounted for observation posts and first line trenches, while howitzers attacked the second and third lines of defence. But no artillery was capable of dealing with the underground burrows and shelters, up to two-thirds of a mile deep, which ran into

Opposite Deadlocked trench warfare earned the name *The Sausage Machine* because it took in men, churned out corpses and stayed firmly screwed in place.

Above A German trench gun in action – gunners crawled from dug-outs to fire at advancing infantry.

Left The landscape suffered – and so did the soldiers. They bravely fought their way through blood, mud and slime.

mountains of slag and clinker. These featured impregnable underground caverns, from which 'fresh' German machine gunners could quickly emerge against an infantry attack.

Come on, British pigs

The plan was that battle should commence on June 28, but bad weather prevented this, and it was three more days before the word was given. Of course, by this time the Germans knew what was going on to the point that they raised

LAND 63

banners and placards announcing: 'Come on, British pigs; we are ready for you.'

On Saturday, July 1, the British attacked at 7.30 on a sultry summer morning. Mainly involved was 5 Corps of General Rawlinson's Fourth Army, with 7 Corps of General Allenby's Third Army on its left. There were 19 divisions allotted to the attack, making 200,000 infantry. There were also nearly 100,000 British artillerymen involved, and these fired 13,000 tons of shells in support on July 1 alone.

On the German side, General Fritz von Below was in command of the Second Army.

At the appointed hour, platoon commanders blew their whistles almost in unison, summoning the largely untrained troops to leave their trenches and brave the smudged, cratered wastes of No Man's Land. A series of extended lines advanced – two paces between men and 100 yards between ranks.

The greatest catastrophe

On the other side, the moment the British barrage eased for the infantry assault, German machine gunners rushed from their dugouts and ran to the nearest shell craters, establishing a line of rapid-fire defence. Their moment soon came when the rapidly-advancing thousands reached the German barbed wire and tragically found it uncut by shells along two-thirds of the front. They were aunt-sallies. There was no way forward, and they could not go back because of the press of line after line behind.

The enemy machine guns opened up and mowed down the British at will. The slaughter was on a scale never seen before or since and it was the greatest single catastrophe of 'the great war'. On that first day of the battle of the Somme, British casualties totalled 57,470, Of these, more than 20,000 died where they lay.

Little ground had been gained. Nothing worthwhile had been achieved. There was no chance of a break-out. Yet the offensive continued on Sunday, July 2 . . . on Monday, July 3 . . . on July 4 . . . . On and on went the battering ram, without finesse and with inevitable useless slaughter at around 10,000 a day, through July, August, September, October and into November.

General Douglas Haig, British commander in chief, ordered his troops to press on 'without intermission'; the Germans observed that the British army were 'lions led by donkeys'; and Colonel Winston Churchill protested that 'the open country towards which we are struggling by inches is utterly devoid of military significance. There is no question of breaking the line, or letting loose the cavalry in the open country behind, or of inducing a general withdrawal of the German armies in the West.'

Left *From left to right General Joffre, Sir Douglas Haig and General Foch decided Allied strategy at the Somme: their recipe – more men, more guns.*

Below *Some of the guns in action. This is a British battery of eight-inch howitzers used for shelling artillery positions, trenches and so on.*

Blood and slime

In the midst of the offensive, but without any attempt at co-ordination, a large French contingent, under General Ferdinand Foch, fought on the right of the British, and were able to advance, where the British could not, before eventually becoming just as stuck in the blood-soaked mud – their casualties equally heavy.

Later, during the 140 days of the Somme, torrential rain played its part. The entire battlefield became a slough where the wounded could disappear into slime in an instant, where attacks were pressed with men wading up to their hips, where men drowned in trenches from sheer weariness. The landscape was murdered, as well as its human moles. And always there were guns, aircraft, balloons, bombs and poison gas.

The brave and the dead

Tales of daring were fed back to the public, and there was bravery in the midst of the filth and stagnancy. But mostly the deeds most worthy of medals were done unseen by the medal-givers. There was also muddle and inefficiency on a massive scale, from the miscalculations of the leaders to the British patrols who lost their way at night and found themselves in German trenches in mistake for their own.

The Somme offensive began as a British push, but before it ended nearly all the Empire had taken part. The South Africans joined in at Delville Wood; the Australians were involved at Pozieres and Warlencourt; the New Zealanders fought bravely to the west of Gueudecourt; the Canadians took over at Pozieres; there were even Indians on horseback south of High Wood.

The long battle petered out on November 19, when the Allies managed to reach the southern half of the Bapaume to Peronne road, having achieved little territorially. It was claimed that Haig's plan had ground down the enemy towards his eventual collapse. The cold figures showed that the Allied casualties totalled some 630,000 against 660,000 on the German side.

Both sides fought a battle of attrition. Here the crews of German 21 cm. howitzers survey the resulting devastation.

CAMBRAI

Mobile armoured warfare exploded at Cambrai, France in 1917. For the first time ever, squadrons of tanks roared towards the German lines, striking terror into the hearts of the defenders, and paving the way for the Panzer thrusts of World War II.

Looming out of the mist the British tanks so frightened the Germans that they christened them 'devil coaches'. At Cambrai, massed squadrons of Mark IVs stormed directly towards the German lines. A great improvement on earlier models that had operated in small numbers from September 1916, the Mark VI carried heavier armour plating and mounted two long-barrelled six-pounders and four machine-guns – the 'female' version had just machine-guns. Its maximum speed was around four miles an hour. The wooden bar above the body could be carried round by the tracks to give leverage in muddy conditions.

At the first battle of Cambrai, on November 20, 1917, no fewer than 324 tanks were used, in circumstances of maximum surprise, and the effect on the Germans was as sensational as if flying saucers had descended. The boost to British morale, on the other hand, was as welcome as it was necessary.

This was the first major engagement for the British invention which was to transform tactical planning on land. Named the 'tank' in development in 1915 as a security precaution, it had appeared briefly in small numbers on the Somme on 15 September, 1916, but few had seen it and little had since been said.

In the winter that followed the long battle of the Somme, the Germans had secretly withdrawn slowly from the river to base themselves on a prepared position some miles behind, known as the Hindenburg Line. Hindenburg and Ludendorff had become joint commanders of the German armies.

Thereafter, the Germans made no great effort on the Western Front in 1917. Secure in the knowledge that they had air superiority, they remained defensive, whereas the Allies embarked on two major and extremely costly offensives – both characteristic failures.

Two mistakes by the Allies

First, the French attacked on the Aisne, to the south of Cambrai between Soissons and Rheims. Security was so bad, the Germans knew the battle orders in advance. The French, under General Robert Nivelle, gained a small part of the heights above the Aisne, but at a terrible cost. There was also a serious mutiny in the French army. Nivelle was replaced by General Philippe Pétain.

Second, the Third Battle of Ypres, or Passchendaele, to the north of Cambrai, began

in July, and was to became the crowning horror of the trench warfare of the Western Front.

In the Ypres salient the most unthinkable conditions prevailed. The drainage system had broken down from continual shell fire, and the entire battlefield was a swamp, blasted and cratered like a moonscape.

Grimly and unfeelingly, Sir Douglas Haig had forced his infantry – British, Canadian and Australian – again and again across this water-logged wasteland. Attack after attack – watched in disbelief by the German supremo, Ludendorff himself – petered out among the mud and blood of the Passchendaele Ridge. Haig had created a treadmill of horror and he kept it going with seeming masochism . . . but from a distance. He never once visited the battlefield.

As the months of slaughter, or 'grinding down' as Haig chose to call it, went on, the Germans were killing three soldiers for every man they lost themselves, but Haig somehow managed to go on finding replacements for his dead. By the time the Ypres fighting had at last died down from sheer mutual exhaustion, the British and their Empire had gained a couple of thousand yards at a cost of 300,000 casualties, 'the flower of our manhood'.

Men of vision

But there were some military men of vision. One was General Sir Julian Byng, who was among the first to grasp the importance of the tank as a weapon. Shortly after General Haig had reluctantly broken off his futile offensive, Byng's Third Army, at the instigation of General Ferdinand Foch, about to become generalissimo, launched the surprise tank attack at Cambrai –

the most important centre of German communications in the West at that time.

The Cambrai plan had been produced by Britain's chief tank expert, Colonel Fuller, and Byng had gone along with him on the idea that it could bring dramatic mobility to the static front, with its grim positional warfare. Both agreed the country chosen was ideal for tanks.

Inevitably, the original plan, prepared in August, 1917, changed considerably in discussion. Inevitably, also, when Haig was told, he would have none of it. He did not have much faith in the tank, which he called 'a useful, if mechanically unreliable supporting weapon, but one that could never be considered a decisive one in its own right'.

Eventually, the pro-tank men presented the Cambrai plan to Haig as 'tanks supporting infantry' in a way that got his grudging sanction on October 13.

300 tanks and 1,000 guns

A week later Byng was ready for the crossing of the Hindenburg Line and the capture of Cambrai. He had assembled six infantry divisions, five cavalry divisions, nine tank battalions and 1,000 guns for the drive. Secrecy had been well maintained, with all tank movements taking place at night.

The day dawned misty and at 0630 hours all the tanks, commanded by General Elles, led six divisions of infantry into No Man's Land, supported above by nearly 300 strafing aircraft. The plan worked with incredible smoothness. The tanks broke through the successive belts of

Tanks needed infantry to back them up. Here men of the 11th Inniskilling Fusiliers advance over the captured German second line near Havrincourt. The Germans thought the line impregnable.

German wire, which were of great strength and depth, so that the English, Scottish and Irish regiments which followed were able to sweep over the enemy's outposts and storm the first defensive system of the Hindenburg Line on the whole front. They then pressed on in the shelter of the tanks, and captured the Hindenburg Support Line more than a mile ahead.

The tanks acted like small animated forts, moving through villages and in effect occupying them. At Lateau Wood, a tank even charged a battery of 5.9 mm artillery, pushed between and amongst them, scattering the crews and capturing the guns.

Haig reports victory

The following day Haig sent a report of the battle to London speaking of an amazing victory. It read:

'Yesterday morning the Third Army, under the command of General the Hon. Sir Julian Byng, delivered a number of attacks between St Quentin and the river Scarpe. These attacks were carried out without previous artillery preparation, and in each case the enemy were completely surprised. Our troops have broken into the enemy's positions to a depth of between four and five miles on a wide front, and have captured several thousand prisoners with a number of guns. At the hour of assault on the principal front of the attack a large number of tanks moved forward in advance of the infantry, and broke through the successive belts of German wire, which were of great depth and strength.

'Following through the gaps made by the tanks, English, Scottish, and Irish regiments swept over the enemy's outposts, and stormed the first defensive system of the Hindenburg Line on the whole front. Our infantry and tanks then pressed on in accordance with programme, and captured the German second system of defence more than a mile beyond. This latter is known as the Hindenburg support line.

'In the course of this advance East-country troops took the hamlet of Bonavis and Lateau Wood after stiff fighting. English rifle regiments

Tanks 'cleared the way' by smashing through barbed wire, opening up the softer defences of the Hindenburg Line.

and light infantry captured La Vacquerie, and the formidable defences of the spur known as Welsh Ridge.

'Other English country troops stormed the village of Ribecourt, and fought their way through Coutlett Wood. Highland Territorial battalions crossed the Grand Ravine and entered Flesquieres, where fierce fighting took place.

'West Riding Territorials captured Havrincourt and the German trench systems north of the village, while Ulster battalions covering the latter's left flank moved northwards up the west bank of the Canal du Nord. Later in the morning our advance was continued, and rapid progress was made at all points.

'English, Scottish, Irish, and Welsh battalions secured the crossings of the canal at Masnieres and captured Marcoing and Neuf Wood. The West Riding troops who had taken Havrincourt made remarkable progress east of the Canal du Nord, storming the villages of Graincourt and Anneux, and with the Ulster troops operating west of the canal carried the whole of the German line northwards to the Bapaume-Cambrai road.

'West Lancashire Territorials broke into the enemy's position east of Epehy, and Irish troops

have captured important sections of the Hindenburg Line between Bullecourt and Fontaine-les-Croisilles. The number of prisoners, guns, and material captured cannot yet be estimated.

'The spell of fine dull weather which favoured our preparations for our attacks broke early yesterday. Heavy rain fell during the night and the weather is now stormy.'

In truth, in the first six hours Byng's army had captured more ground than 51 British divisions had done at Third Ypres in four months of desperate fighting.

The tanks had driven at will through the German lines to a distance of 10,000 yards.

As British tanks advance towards the attack on Bourlon Wood, they pass German guns already captured in earlier attacks. The Germans lost 142 guns and a total of 50,000 killed, missing or wounded.

The terrifying tank

On the German side it was a traumatic experience. The tank has become known as a blitzkreig weapon of great versatility – as flamethrower, mine-exploder, cavalry recce vehicle, armoured amphibian, mobile destroyer and so on – but it terrified the Germans at Cambrai. Many crossed themselves and surrendered on their knees.

It must have been utterly unnerving for them to be faced, without warning or explanation, by steel monsters which crushed vast wire entanglements, like so much straw, crashed through dugouts, smashed machine-guns to bits, and ploughed on across the mud with flames darting from their steaming exhaust pipes.

Nearly 9,000 German prisoners and 100 German guns were captured that day and British losses were comparatively negligible. And one of the strongest sectors of the German Western Front had been broken in a single blow.

Ludendorff was beside himself. The surprise of the event completely shattered him. He frantically ordered up several divisions for a counter-attack. But he was grimly aware that this would take a week or so to stage.

In fact, he need not have worried. Haig who, earlier in the year, had so confidently assembled his cavalry behind the Ypres swamps for the expected easy victory ride to the coast, had had no expectation of success with Byng's tanks, and had concentrated no reserves to exploit success in front of Cambrai. Indeed, most of the troops he should have used were rotting in the Passchendaele mud.

By November 29, Ludendorff was ready. His counter-attack was completely successful. By the next day the British had lost all and more of the ground they had won in the great massed tank victory of November 20.

Top left *Tanks line up ready to advance.*

Left *Defenders at Cambrai found rifles and grenades useless before the terrifying tanks – but the Germans were developing anti-tank flame-throwers and guns.*

Right *In six hours, 324 tanks captured more ground than 51 division had taken in four months of fighting at Ypres.*

Cambrai

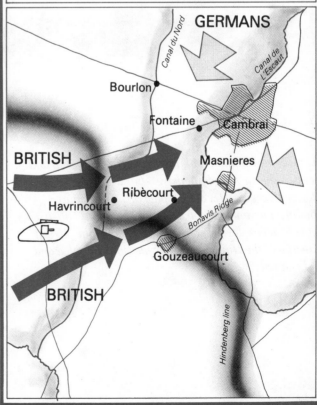

GAZALA

In the deserts of North Africa, during the drive on Tobruk in 1942, Rommel displayed the fast-moving tactical brilliance that has made his campaigns famous — if the British had read his book on tank warfare they might have made fewer mistakes.

At Gazala, Rommel took the initiative. Churchill had pressed for an Allied offensive – but while they prepared, Rommel struck. His daring paid off. As he poured forward the tanks, troop carriers, armoured half-tracks, Kubelwagens, lorries, and motorcycles of the Afrika Korps and the Italians, the Gazala line crumbled and Tobruk fell.

Many of the British troops who took part in the Battle of Gazala in the Western Desert were 'militiamen'. They had been called up three years before, in the summer of 1939, simply because they were 20 years of age. After training, they had been shipped out to the desert to fight the Italians. They were the 'brave amateurs' of World War II – muddling through to win in the end.

Below *The mighty 88 was the wonder-gun of the Desert War. With the base dug in, the gun presented a small target to tanks and could pierce 99 mm. armour at 2,200 yards. It was highly accurate and the Germans deployed it with skill, forming an anti-tank screen behind which armour could operate. The 25-foot long gun could throw an 88 mm. shell nearly 11,000 yards at a rate of six a minute.*

So ill-prepared had the cavalry arm of the British Army been at the start of the war that some regiments in the desert had only horses and swords with which to harry the Italians. Nor had things improved all that much by the summer of 1942.

Reconnaissance regiments – vital in desert warfare – were equipped with South African made armoured cars that had been used in World War I, or with Rolls-Royce, Daimler and Humber vehicles of similar vintage. Tank regiments had mainly slow, obsolete Valentines or stop-gap Honeys. Virtually all the armoured cars and tanks in use had 'pea-shooter' guns, known as two-pounders.

There were a few American Grant tanks at Gazala, with larger 75mm guns but these were in

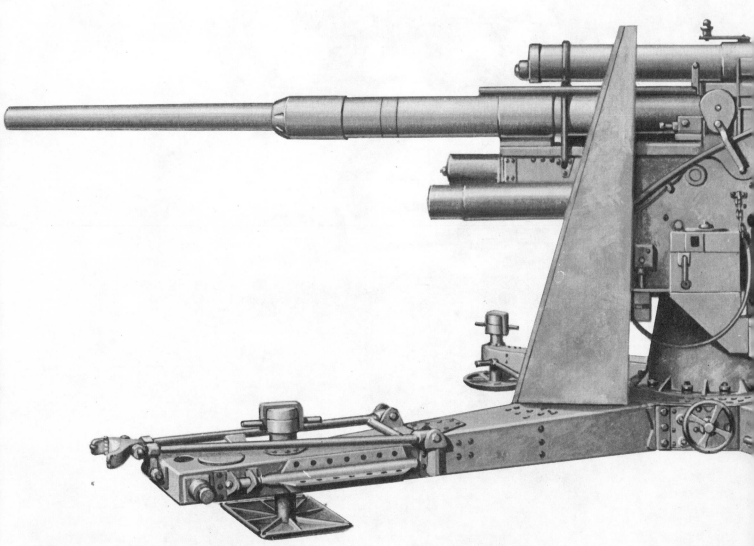

Left The British 25-pounder gun-howitzer formed part of the perimeter defences of Tobruk. It fired a 3.45-inch shell over 13,000 yards at a rate between 12 and 15 a minute.

Below A gun crew of the RHA in action on the perimeter. The 25-pounders were reliable and effective – but ammunition was low.

fixed turrets; and the Grant, which could not 'cruise', was vulnerable and liable to break down.

The mighty 88

All tanks in Rommel's Africa Korps could outgun almost anything the British possessed. His Panzer Mark IIIs and Mark IVs had 75mm guns (or 50mm at worst) and adaptations were appearing with 88mm – the finest gun of the war. These could knock out British armour at 1,500 yards; British two-pounder shells bounced off

German armour at anything over 1,000 yards. This was like David taking on Goliath, but with both hands tied behind his back until the last moment. Rings of German anti-tank guns – also 88mm – wrought similar havoc.

Not only was British armour outgunned and outpaced; it also tended to 'brew up'. Auxiliary 40-gallon drums of high-octane fuel, to give range, were often strapped to the flanks of the tank or armoured car. Incendiary bullets could cause an instant inferno from which no crewman could hope to escape. Charred bones in black-ened iron 'coffins' were grim symbols of this phase of the desert war.

Such was life as the British Eighth Army, commanded by Lieutenant-General Neil Ritchie, faced the Africa Korps, and its Italian allies, under Field Marshal Erwin Rommel, the Desert Fox.

Gazala, point of no return

Germany dominated the central Mediterranean at this time and had good port facilities for the desert campaign. The two thorns in her flesh were Malta, whence her shipping was harried, and Tobruk, the Eighth Army's only nearby supply port. These were Hitler's two objectives in the area in the early part of 1942.

But Gazala, 40 miles to the west of Tobruk, was a sort of point of no return for both sides, half-way across the bleak deserts of Cyrenaica, in the centre of the long Mediterranean coast of Africa; their land supply and communication lines were stretched to the maximum.

Building up to battle

So, for the first few months of 1942, Rommel halted on the Tmimi-Mechili Line, facing Gazala until he could reinforce – notably with replacement Panzers through Tripoli.

During this same period Ritchie, a com-

The British defence was a series of 'boxes' which fought virtually independently, holding off attacks until supplies ran out.

paratively inexperienced staff officer thrust into the breach by Auchinleck, who preferred to command from Cairo, was building a strong Gazala Line. This consisted of a series of defended boxes – based on the British 'square' of Waterloo fame, but adapted to armoured fighting – linked to a vast minefield that stretched southwards from the sea to the Bir Hacheim Foreign Legion fortress. Each 'box' was garrisoned by an artillery-supported brigade group.

The desert war up to that point had been one of shuttling see-saw successes – three to each side. Rommel had been the latest to advance to reconquer the western half of Cyrenaica. Now he was building up to take Tobruk, without which, he knew, the British would have to retreat to the Egyptian frontier. Meanwhile, attempts were to be made by other German forces to capture the island of Malta.

The British plan was that the Eighth Army would attack, when ready, from the boxes of the Gazala line. In fact, Rommel struck first, on May 27.

On paper both sides were fairly matched: about 130,000 men and just over 700 tanks each.

The lesson of the Desert Fox

At first, it went fairly well for Britain, with Rommel frustrated in his break-through attempts for five days. One of the factors was a new anti-tank gun Britain was trying out, a useful six-pounder, nearer in bore to the German 88s. The RAF, too, was attacking every German supply convoy.

But losses of British tanks were heavy, partly because Ritchie failed to keep the two armoured divisions – the 1st and the 7th – together. He evidently had not read Rommel's tank lectures. 'If the enemy is foolish enough to allow any

The big guns of the defence pound the German positions. But with the British tank forces scattered and picked-off surrender was inevitable.

scattering of his tank forces,' the Fox had written, 'it will be easy to destroy them piecemeal.'

The 7th Armoured Division, the famous Desert Rats, suffered heavy casualties when its brigades were fighting separately, on orders from the top, instead of together.

As time went on, the British became concerned to defend their vast stores at a railhead that had been built at Belhamed. But Ritchie failed sufficiently to co-ordinate his forces for adequate counter-attack, or even to build up a clear picture of what was going on.

Rommel breaks through

Rommel meanwhile had carried out a right hook around the minefields, and had secured his rear by forcing a gap through the mines at Trigh Capuzzo, in case he had to withdraw west. He has also sent mobile columns to take Bir Hacheim from Koenig's brave Free French. Its defence was the first sign of a revival in French fighting vitality since the 1940 debacle.

Gazala and Tobruk

Tobruk Perimeter

British Minefields

Ain el Gazala

Tobruk

BRITISH

Acroma

Pilastrino

ROMMEL'S ADVANCE

'Knightsbridge'

El Adem

'The Cauldron'

Mediterranean Sea

Bir Hakeim

AFRICA

FREE FRENCH TROOPS

On the night of June 4, the British attacked through the minefields in an area nicknamed The Cauldron. One South African division was standing by, together with both armoured divisions. The Cauldron attack was abortive and unnecessarily expensive. By nightfall, 60 British tanks were destroyed, and the ground troops annihilated or routed. Four regiments of field artillery were also lost.

On June 10 news came through that Bir Hacheim had fallen at last, and the Gazala Line was cut in two. At this stage, Rommel had about 150 first-line tanks left, plus 60 inferior Italian ones, to Britain's 180, so the numbers were fairly even.

On June 11, Rommel drove out towards a direct attack on Tobruk. On that day, on a bloody, sand-stormed, fire-raked battlefield, by a 'box' known as Knightsbridge (because gentlemen guardsmen who spent their time in that area of London had been holding it) the rest of the British armour was outgunned and destroyed.

Tobruk's South African defenders could hold out only until June 20, when the port fell, 33,000 prisoners with it.

Ritchie gave the order: 'Abandon the Gazala Line' and the British withdrew to a depression known as Alamein while Malta held-out stubbornly towards her George Cross.

Left Rommel directed his forces with skill and energy forcing the Allies to fight on the retreat.

Below left The sweep to Tobruk, through successful, was held up by the Gazala minefield, the Free French at Bir Hakeim and dogged resistance at Knightsbridge.

Below A German gun crew in action. Rommel's tactics were to keep his tanks together, protected by artillery, and launch a series of concentrated attacks.

STALINGRAD

At Stalingrad, Russia in 1942, Hitler, threw his military machine against the resistance of an embattled people. In one of the greatest battles of all time, the million-strong Soviet Army lured the Wehrmacht into a trap then swooped down and annihilated it unit by unit.

Hitler had no-one to blame but himself for the situation the Wehrmacht, the German army, got itself into at Stalingrad, when it sustained its greatest-ever defeat. Up to Moscow, and the nightmare winter of 1941–42, all had gone as planned. The Moscow crisis had been an interruption, not an end, to Hitler's run of strategic successes. A new year meant a new life-force. So ran his tantrums.

His political and military strategy for 1942 was final. It called for the defeat of Soviet forces in the south, the conquest of the Caucasus, an advance to the Volga River, and the seizure of Stalingrad. These were the strangling fingers that would throttle the USSR as a state. The swift seizure of the Caucasian oilfields alone would bring the Soviet war machine to a standstill; and on all fronts, he *knew*, the Russian reserves had been exhausted.

So ran Hitler's visionary dream.

Hitler's impossible dream

In truth, on the German side of the Russian fronts, what with the bitter winters, the failure to anticipate them, the long supply lines, the exhaustion of the troops, the decline in reserves, and other factors, it was the impossible dream. But no-one could tell this to the German dictator. He treated his advisors with contempt. His god-like trances became more numerous.

Hitler had always believed that victory was a matter of will-power, and had proved it by carrying to success plans all others had condemned. And certainly, by June 1942, it must have seemed, to all around him, that Hitler was right once more.

The Wehrmacht was cruising fast and freely to the Caucasus and had destroyed 300,000 Soviet troops at Kharkov and Kiev in three armies; the Japanese were over-running the Far East, and looked like linking soon in the drive against the USSR; the Eighth Army were in headlong retreat towards the Egyptian border; King Farouk was preparing to welcome Mussolini at Alexandria; there had been no Allied invasion of Europe.

*German soldiers **left** fought Russian infantry and guerillas **right** inch by inch through Stalingrad's wilderness of broken buildings.*

The road to Stalingrad

Elated and confident, Hitler set his forces on the road to Stalingrad, in an 'inspired' move to gain the ultimate conquest in the east before the Allies were ready to open the promised 'second front' in the west. He had gambled on a short sharp war in eastern Europe, and that was what it had to be.

Hitler's hatred of Soviet Russia transcended all his other hatreds. But he had to settle them soon. All his writings had warned against fighting on two fronts at once. Not even he could split his will-power for such a situation.

So the USSR had to be brought quickly to heel. There were ideological compulsions, as well as strategic ones. In *Mein Kampf*, Hitler had summed up his greatest dream, thus: 'When we speak of new territory to take, we must first think of Russia. Destiny itself points the way there.'

In the mid-summer of 1942, Stalin, Soviet supreme commander as well as dictator, expected a new Nazi thrust on Moscow, from the Bryansk area. Instead, the Wehrmacht struck south again and took the naval base of Sebastopol on the tip of the Crimea. Having completed the conquest of the famous peninsula, they freed a whole army for use elsewhere, some divisions of which began to drive, with blitzkrieg speed, towards the Don River bend and Stalingrad, adding to the threat of Russia being cut in two, if the Volga was taken.

Stalin at once reorganized his forces and sent some of his most trusted political leaders to the front at Stalingrad. They included such famous names as Malenkov, Kruschev and Malychev.

Stalin chooses Zhukov

But still the Nazis drove forward, and, on August 27, 1942, the ruthless but simplistic Marshal Georgi Konstantinovich Zhukov, victor of Moscow – and perhaps the greatest soldier of the century – was summoned from the Western Front and named Deputy Supreme Commander-in-Chief, to Stalin. It was a measure of Zhukov's standing that there never had been a deputy supreme commander before, and there never would be again.

Stalingrad's fate, inseperable from Russia's, was placed in Zhukov's hands – and rough, strong hands they were.

Zhukov's style of leadership was simple. He had to be obeyed absolutely. There was nothing refined or likeable about him. He was a bull-like man, who would issue near-impossible orders, accompanied by the simple command: 'Do it now, or face the firing squad.' Nor were they empty words. Officers and men were indeed shot at his whim.

There was a constancy, as well as a simplicity, about Zhukov's tactics of necessity throughout the war. In non-urban areas, he subscribed wholeheartedly to the traditional Russian ploy: trade space for time. Otherwise, even in cramped

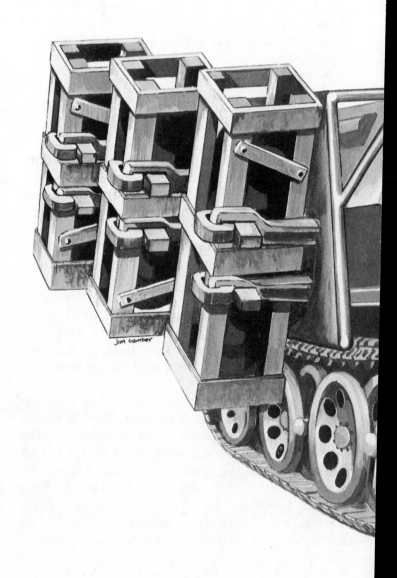

Jim bamber

STALINGRAD

Shifting embattled 'freedom fighters' from buildings they knew well took special weapons. The German Sdkfz 251/1 was a half-track troop carrier carrying six adjustable racks designed to hold and fire 28 or 32 cm. rockets direct from their packing crates. In use, the rocket carrier could be driven close to an occupied building and was aimed by pointing the entire vehicle.

WH - 154297

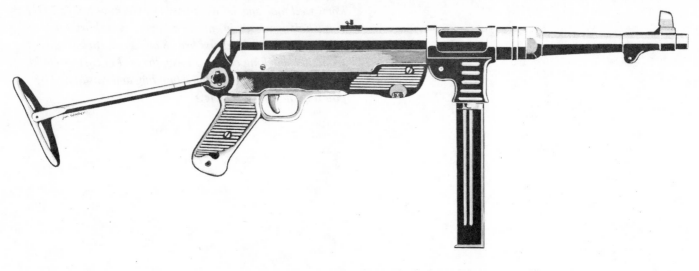

Close-quarter fighting required close-quarter weapons.

Above left *The German ERMA MP40 submachine gun was exactly suited to fast-moving, near hand-to-hand fighting. Its folding stock and plastic fore-grip combined lightness with strength and gave it high combat effectiveness. The submachine gun took a 32-shot magazine and fired 9 mm. bullets at the rate of 500 a minute.*

Left As a German infantry man smashes his way into a sniper's hide-out a submachine gunner stands ready.

Above The PPSL-41 was the Russian equivalent to the MP40. The drum magazine took 71 rounds of 7.62 mm. ammunition and the cyclic rate of fire was 900 a minute.

Below In fighting at the approaches to Stalingrad, the Russian defenders made full use of the submachine gun.

circumstances, he believed in letting the enemy extend themselves; he would wait until the last moment of offensive momentum and would then grind them down in rough, bloody, interlocking encounters as they neared their objective, while holding back substantial reserves for a speedy, powerful counter-attack, the moment he judged the enemy strength to be all-but spent. In the process, he did not care how many lives he sacrificed, as long as he won in the end.

The opposing forces that summer, along the entire eastern front, from the Barents Sea to the Black Sea, were slightly in Germany's favour numerically – and so weighty as scarcely to be comprehensible to any but the top-brass.

With defenders as fanatical as those at Stalingrad every inch of cover counted when moving into position.

Snipers by day, grenades and Molotov cocktails by night – the Germans had to guard against vicious attacks 24 hours a day.

Six million men in battle

The Axis powers had 217 divisions and 20 brigades, of which 178 divisions, eight brigades and four air forces were German. This represented 80 per cent of the total Nazi forces.

The Wehrmacht totalled six million men (including 800,000 allied troops), 3,250 tanks and self-propelled guns, 55,000 guns and mortars; and the eastern Luftwaffe had 3,500 planes.

But the new factor in mid-1942 was that the front was now so wide as to produce a reduction in operational density everywhere, despite the incredible numerical totals.

In an effort to prevent the Germans from reaching the Volga River, Stalin had, on July 12, set up a new Stalingrad Front, instead of the overall South-western Command. This was obvious but sensible anticipation. Directive No. 45, of the German High Command, dated July 23 ordered Army Group B and the Fourth Air Force to seize Stalingrad and gain a stronghold on the Volga River. This would give victory by cutting off the oil-rich Caucasus from the rest of the Soviet Union.

Within a few weeks, the Stalingrad Front consisted of 38 divisions, of low strength (perhaps equivalent to 18 normal divisions). The total front strength was 190,000 men, 350 tanks, 340 planes and 8,000 guns or mortars.

Against this, Germany was attacking Stalingrad with 250,000 men, 750 tanks, 1,200 planes, and 7,500 guns or mortars.

The Germans break through

On July 26, German armour broke through the Soviet defenses in the Don River bend and reached the river, and on August 23, the German Sixth Army and the Fourth Panzer Army, both under the command of General Friedrich Paulus, broke through again at the same point and cut the Stalingrad sector in two, before reaching the vitally important supply waterway, the Volga itself, just north of Stalingrad. This resulted in the Russian Stalingrad Front being divided. The part cut off, including Stalingrad proper, became known as the South-east Front. The German advance had succeeded in the centre partly because most of the Soviet strength was still on the flanks. But Paulus had not paused to wipe out Russian pockets as he stormed forward, so that Russia was able to retain bridgeheads on the right bank of the Don, as well as an important foothold west of Serafimovitch. This meant Paulus's flanks were weaker than he realized.

Meanwhile hundreds of German bombers were keeping up non-stop raids on the city of Stalingrad, in which its factories and much of its housing were reduced to grim demolition sites or to rubble. Thousands of civilians died in the raids.

The city's famous tractor plant, in the northern outskirts, was attacked by the Wehrmacht, but factory workers defended it without fear for their lives, and the attack was temporarily repulsed. Meanwhile strong diversionary Soviet efforts on other fronts drew off some of the reserves intended for Stalingrad.

As Zhukov conferred with Stalin, before taking complete control on August 27, it was learned that the Wehrmacht had crossed the Don in force, and were at the city named after Stalin. Advancing on a broad front, Paulus had succeeded, by the evening of August 23, in driving his Sixth Army left through the northern outskirts, to the right bank of the Volga. And within two weeks, the Fourth Panzer Army would cut an opening to the river through the southern suburbs, whereupon Hitler would impress on Paulus that the rest of the city had to be taken, and the armies joined, without delay.

Meanwhile, Stalin and Zhukov had moved everything they could, except for the newly-formed strategic reserves, intended for a subsequent counter-offensive, into the Stalingrad area for the coming crunch on which so much depended.

'Comrade, kill your German'

In Stalingrad, the population set about joining its defending troops in making the invader's positions as untenable as cunning and bravery would allow. 'Comrade, kill your German' became the universal catchphrase. In the wilderness of broken buildings, Russian infantry or guerillas sniped at any member of the German Sixth Army foolish enough to leave his trench or billet. Grenades were tossed into any Nazi dugouts or premises that could be reached in darkness and Molotov cocktails (bottles of petrol with simple wick fuses, as used by rebels to this day) crashed on vehicles by the hour. Also, night after night, until the river froze over in November, supplies and reinforcements were smuggled across in small boats.

The garrison and the civilians defended the ruins of central Stalingrad, street by street, house by house, and won the astonished admiration of the free world. As the German Sixth Army tried again and again to quell this resistance, once and for all, they little knew that Zhukov was assembling, in two groups of six armies, a million men, 800 tanks and 10,000 guns for the Stalingrad counter offensive. By the middle of November the Soviets had eight armies on the Don-Volga front.

The Russians counter-attack

In Stalingrad and the adjoining areas of the Don and the Volga, in the wearing-down period of the summer and autumn of 1942, the Nazis had already lost three-quarters of a million men, 900 tanks, 1,800 guns and 1,500 planes. They were being reinforced by unreliable Italians, Rumanians and Hungarians. But Hitler was confident they could quell any counter-attack in November, hold Stalingrad and then release troops for taking the Caucasian oilfields as planned. After all, did not Germany by November, 1942 occupy no less than 750,000 square miles of Russia – an area with a pre-war population of 80 million? And was not Goebbels telling the world every day the truth that the German race was infinitely superior to all other races?

On November 19 and 20, the Russian counter-attack, in the rear of the German forces at Stalingrad, was launched on a scale never seen before anywhere. Again, in numbers, there was not much to choose between Slav and Teuton on the general Stalingrad Front. But where Russian weapons had been getting better, the Wehrmacht had little new to offer in offence or defence. It was the same old weapons in the same old well-rehearsed highly-professional routines.

The Rumanian Third Army was devoured in record time, and the Soviet soldiers then fell upon the left of the Sixth Army, the Rumanian Fourth Army and the Fourth Panzer Army, which had failed to relieve the Stalingrad Germans. Once both Rumanian armies had succumbed, Soviet armour was able to race through and attack the Sixth Army's rear, capturing the bridge it used for its supplies en route.

In just over four days, the Russians captured

250,000 Axis troops in and to the west of Stalingrad, having smashed two broad holes in either flank of the huge salient before the city.

Paulus was then about to attempt to fight his way out of the city to the south-west with what was left of his army, but Hitler had other ideas. Goering had promised to fly in 500 tons of supplies a day to Stalingrad's two airports, and the Fuehrer gave the order to Paulus to remain and continue fighting for the city.

Air deliveries to Stalingrad fell hopelessly below Goering's promises, and were as little as 20 to 30 tons a day instead of 500. Meanwhile Stalingrad guerillas were blowing up stores as they arrived, while those without dynamite derailed trains or set fire to lorries.

Before Zhukov's massive forces had closed the noose completely around the Sixth Army, Paulus could have linked up with another German army, Manstein's 6th Armoured division, which had forced itself to within 25 miles of the city. But Paulus dithered and finally decided a break-out was not feasible.

Meanwhile, part of the Luftwaffe had been withdrawn to defend Tunisia against the British and Americans, so Paulus got less and less support or help from the air.

By January 8, Zhukov had completed the stranglehold and called on Paulus to surrender. Somehow, with his starving and fearful army, he held on until January 30. But then the Russian armies broke into the centre of Stalingrad, from north-west and west, amidst incredible scenes of rejoicing among the city's remaining population. The next day, the newly-promoted tall, gaunt Field Marshal Paulus capitulated, with 25 other generals and the remnants of his army. Their march to Zhukov's head-quarters led them through mounds of German bodies which new snow was mercifully covering.

Since November 19, 32 divisions and three brigades had been destroyed completely, while the remaining 16 divisions of the Wehrmacht had lost up to 75 per cent of their strength. Total German losses in the Don, Volga and Stalingrad sectors had totalled one and a half million men, together with nearly six months' arms production in the Reich.

Russia had broken Hitler's spell. Even non-blind Nazis could see for the first time their 'invicible' party and leader were frail and human. For the first time since the 1930s a dark cloud had appeared foreshadowing things to come.

Stalingrad

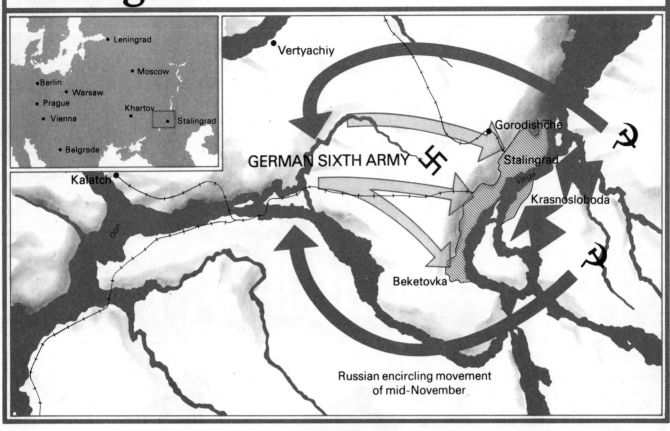

Leningrad

Moscow

Berlin
Warsaw
Prague
Vienna
Khartov
Stalingrad
Belgrade

Vertyachiy

Gorodishche

GERMAN SIXTH ARMY

Stalingrad

Volga

Kalatch

Krasnosloboda

Don

Beketovka

Russian encircling movement
of mid-November

Below *After six months hard fighting the Red Flag flies over Stalingrad again. The German losses totalled one and a half million men: Stalingrad had become a decisive turning point of World War II.*

Above *Marshall Zhukov sucked the Germans into Stalingrad, making them fight all the way, and then fell upon Paulus's Sixth Army, forcing it to surrender and taking the strategic initiative for the Soviets.*

Hitler believed the capture of Stalingrad would compensate for the defeat before Moscow in the disastrous winter of 1941–42. But the German war machine was over-stretched and although the advance to Stalingrad went well at first, under the severe conditions of a Russian winter the Wehrmacht faced a better-equipped opponent.

CASSINO AND ANZIO

In the theatrical setting of the Italian mountains in 1944, the Allies fought doggedly to shift the Germans from their eyrie atop Monte Cassino. At Anzio and in assaults on the peak itself Allied forces combined to achieve the breakthrough.

Observation is the key to a modern land battle, and Italy's Monte Cassino was an eyrie from which young eagle-eyed Germans were able for months to direct artillery or air arm fire on anything that moved in the two wide valleys which met at right angles below. This was a classic case where the battleground shaped the battle.

Cassino itself was a market town of 25,000 inhabitants, sited between the Rapido river valley and the steep massif behind. It stood, and stands, about halfway between Naples and Rome. It had begun its life as Casinum about the third or fourth century B.C., and it had been fought over many times since then, for the very good reason that it is one of the most perfect defensive positions in Europe, a natural barrier between northern and southern Italy.

Through its 1,700 foot high mountain, Cassino

Below Allied artillery, here an American 57 mm. anti-tank unit had to winkle out **right** *the German defence, here a light anti-aircraft gun, from well dug-in positions on Monte Cassino.*

Infantry took the brunt of the fighting at Monte Cassino and the .303-inch Bren was their standard light machine gun. Effective up to 800 yards, it could fire the 30 rounds in the magazines at a rate of 500 a minute.

had another outstanding claim to fame. It was atop Monte Cassino that the monk Benedict had founded the Benedictine Order in the sixth century, and a massive abbey had been established there ever since, poised and erect against the awe-inspiring backdrop of the Appenines which rose tier upon tier into the magic of the cloud-capped snowline.

Hitler forecasts wrong

After Rommel and his armies had been swept from Africa, it was obvious that the Allies would maintain the momentum of their success. But, not for the first time, Hitler mis-read Churchill and moved defensive forces to the Balkans. Even when, early in September 1943, the British Eighth Army and the Fifth American Army (half of it British) landed in the east, at Taranto in the foot curve of Italy, and at Salerno, in the west, near Naples, respectively, Hitler thought this to be a bluff to cover the real objective – the Balkans.

Notwithstanding the Fuehrer's theory, Field-marshal Albert Kesselring, who had read his history books, kept his strength up in Italy, and immediately prepared a plan by which he would lead the Allies by stages to Monte Cassino, to hold them there.

Kesselring picks his ground

Italy, with its backbone of mountains, had always been a country in which the defender chose the battlefield, and Kesselring made no mistake in his choice. At Cassino, the Allies would have no room to manoeuvre, and, unless the mountain fell, Rome was safe. To overcome this natural barrier by a frontal attack would be costly in the extreme.

But for extra insurance, Kesselring entrusted the defence line to the mainly young and fearless troops of the 14th Panzer Corps of the Tenth Army, under General von Senger und Etterlin.

The Cassino decision having been taken in good time – when the Fifth Army was 60 miles to the south – General von Senger was able to blast emplacements in the mountain's granite, set machine gun nests behind rocky outcrops and construct mortar emplacements in the safety of gullies. The mountainsides were then sown with mines and protected with barbed wire. Trip wires attached to flares and mines were placed at all

Above *Commanders at Cassino from left to right, General Dwight D. Eisenhower, Lt.-Gen. Richard L. McCreery and Lt.-Gen. Mark W. Clark.*

Below *The German Nebelwerfer launched 150 mm. rockets – one at a time to prevent the weapon overturning – and took a minute and a half to reload. The rockets weighed about 70 pounds and had a range of 7,000 yards.*

possible approaches. All key positions were reinforced with steel and concrete. A network of tunnels was created, and the town of Cassino heavily fortified. Finally, the Rapido was dammed so that, when the rains came, the entire valley would become a sea of mud, marsh and water. Only the Monastery was left untouched.

Mud and mountains

To allow plenty of time, the rearguards had delayed and nibbled at the Fifth Army, under General Mark Clark, making them fight for every river and hill in the approaches. Three vital months were gained this way, while Clark's men forded the Volturno and Biferno rivers and tackled Monte Camino, a smaller mountain before Cassino.

The Eighth Army meanwhile, having advanced some 600 miles up the Adriatic side of the Italian peninsula and having bravely crossed four rivers, culminating in the formidable Sangro, was stuck in the mud and the mountains, where it would have to remain for the rest of the winter. It lost its inspiration, too, when General Montgomery left to take charge of the invasion of France and was succeeded by General Sir Oliver Leese.

The Eighth and Fifth Armies were both responsible to General Sir Harold Alexander, as commander in chief of the land forces.

The Italians had, by this time, deserted their Axis partners and some were already fighting alongside the Allies, as part of the surrender agreement.

The main purpose of the landings had not been to subdue all Italy but to capture her airfields and use them against Germany. Those in the south fell quickly and came into use. But Eisenhower was determined there should be no delay in taking those in the north (as well as the psychologically important city of Rome) to help in softening up German positions in France for the Normandy landings. But dates had to be revised again and again, as the Fifth Army regularly threw itself against the mountain only to be promptly thrown back.

No amount of shelling and bombing had had any apparent effect on the defenders. Tanks, too, proved themselves useless. Large numbers had been landed, but mostly they lay by the roadsides or among the olive groves.

The troops of the Fifth Army involved in seeking to climb Benedict's mountain were Americans (of all colours and persuasions) British, Canadians, Poles, Indians, French, Moroccans, and New Zealanders. They tried everything they knew, and mules suffered with them, carrying ammunition, but to little effect. The one splendid thing, from a wider Allied point of view, was that the attacking armies had attracted to Germany's southern front many valuable divi-

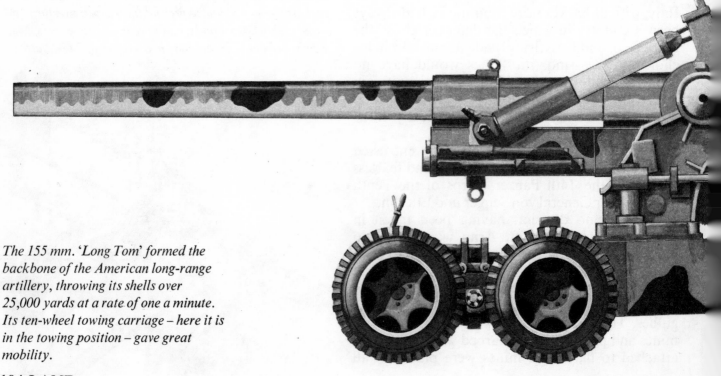

The 155 mm. 'Long Tom' formed the backbone of the American long-range artillery, throwing its shells over 25,000 yards at a rate of one a minute. Its ten-wheel towing carriage – here it is in the towing position – gave great mobility.

sions that Hitler could have used elsewhere.

Flower of the Hitler Youth

But as week followed weary week, into January, more and more lives were lost with absolutely nothing in the way of progress to show for it. One of the reasons was that members of the 1st German Parachute Division were the main suicidal defenders of Cassino. These were Hitler's brainwashed, insensitive bulls – the fanatical products of his master-race youth programme. They had been brought up, from childhood, to believe their lives to be dedicated to the Fuehrer. Normally the toughest of hill positions would have fallen to the tough New Zealanders. But even they died in vain on the mountainside. Blind fanatical faith in the shape of blonde young Aryans beat them back each time. The Hitler-youths were as eager to die for Fascism on Cassino as the Japanese suicide pilots. Their bunkers enabled them to wait underground during the barrages, and then they would emerge to die in bunches attacking from and defending the machine gun positions.

Day after endless day; night after endless night, the Fifth Army gave all it had in the most appalling conditions of snow, frost and slimy mud. But the natural fortress sanctuary and its fervid fighting moles did them down every time.

*Top Bombing raids left the monastery atop Monte Cassino in ruins but **below** the infantry still had to winkle out defenders from their fortified emplacements and a network of tunnels. Americans, British, Canadians, French, Indians, New Zealanders and Poles gave their lives clearing the slopes of Monte Cassino.*

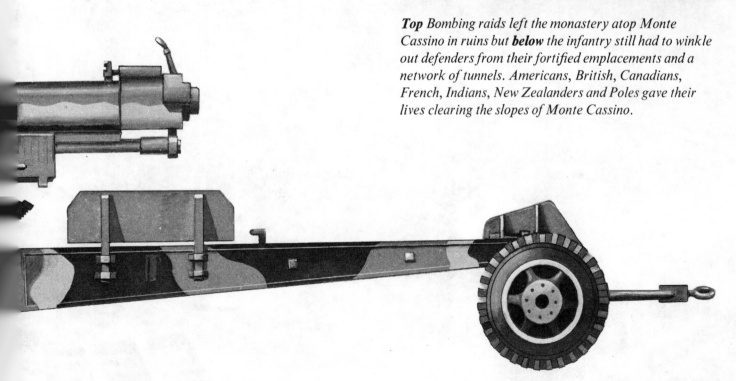

To shift Kesselring's Hitler Youth from their defensive
positions around Cassino, the Allies had virtually to lay
the area waste. Here the mountain looms over a destroyed
bridge and a knocked out tank. Ironically the rubble
proved a major obstacle to the Allied attack.

Landing at Anzio

Meanwhile, a seaborne landing behind the enemy's lines had moved from being one plan for Italy to being *the* new plan for taking Rome. Instead of smashing head on endlessly against the steep mountain, it seemed suddenly sensible to take him in the rear. As soon as enough landing craft were available, in the last days of January, 50,000 Allied troops with 5,000 vehicles went ashore on the gently graded beaches at Anzio, 80 miles north of Cassino and just 30 miles south of the eternal city. The immediate aim was to move east and cut the German supply routes, while the Fifth Army launched an all-out attack on Cassino. This would catch the bulk of the German forces in Italy in a nutcracker. There would be an attempted withdrawal in a panic from the mountains. The march on Rome could then proceed with haste, but with ease.

At first all went well at Anzio – too well. The landing was almost bloodless. Surprise was complete. The sad result was nobody tried to move ahead of schedule. Everyone waited through day one until day two brought the next scheduled moves. Meanwhile, Kesselring was rapidly moving troops down from Rome while reinforcing the Cassino area. Withdrawal apparently never entered his head.

Like their brothers at Cassino, the Allied troops at Anzio were overlooked – in their case from the Alban hills. Kesselring knew that observation was the key to any modern land battle. The Allies could have taken these hills on the first day. They were to suffer a long time for their lack of initiative.

Bloody stalemate

The bridgehead was soon surrounded; there was now no chance to break out and link with the Fifth Army. On both fronts it was a dreadful and bloody stalemate. All through the spring, Alexander tried everything. Eventually, he regrouped,

The American bridge head at Anzio, here 'Ducks' of the Fifth Army come ashore, was soon surrounded by the Germans and bloody stalemate descended on both fronts.

and drew from the best of the Eighth Army to buttress the Fifth for yet another 'decisive' attack on the Nazi mountain. Even when the bombing of the Monastery itself was sanctioned, after the monks had been advised on the radio to leave, no improvement was achieved.

Meanwhile, 80 miles to the north, an immense strain was put upon the Allied shipping which supplied and supported Anzio, and which was urgently wanted for the invasion of France. And over the beachhead, the Luftwaffe, with airfields galore nearby, had the edge over the RAF and the American Air Force.

With the 'Overlord' invasion scheduled for early June, it was imperative that Alexander should somehow succeed in Italy in May, and so release promised divisions for the main assault on Fortress Europe.

The final thrust

Early in May, the reinforced Allies had a two to one superiority in numbers over the Germans at Cassino, and could call on almost overwhelming air support. Heavy bombing of the strong areas immediately behind the mountain helped to isolate the German forces in the front of Cassino.

Alexander's imperative May attack went in, with immense weight, on the night of May 11. By sheer volume of artillery and air fire, and through the massed infantry of the Fifth and Eighth Armies, fairly rapid progress was made in the first hours; and, although enemy resistance stiffened, once surprise was over, the Allies superior fire power eventually prevailed.

By the third day, the two Allied armies had broken through to the main road to Rome, below Monte Cassino, and, early on May 18, Polish troops stormed the summit of the mountain to clear the last Nazi fanatics from around the ruined Monastery.

On May 25, nearly nine months after the first landing, the Fifth Army made contact with the Anzio invaders, and on June 4 the Allies entered Rome.

Two days later, Normandy was invaded.

Cassino blocked the Allied route through Italy, an out-flanking landing at Anzio got nowhere. Opening the road to Rome took massive reinforcements and overwhelming air bombardment.

Cassino

BATTLE OF THE BULGE

Towards the end of 1944, Hitler tried for the ultimate grand slam with a Panzer drive through Luxembourg and the Ardennes. The counter-offensive, under Eisenhower, Montgomery and Patton, produced some of the toughest fighting of the war.

American Sherman tanks wait before going into action at the Battle of the Bulge.

Hitler was always a passionate advocate of the offensive as the only way to win, so it should have been obvious, when the Fuehrer had his back to the wall, in December, 1944, he would counter-attack.

But the Allies were flushed with success; their intelligence was misreading the German dispositions; and there were serious divisions between America and British opinion on how the war should be finished off quickly.

Field Marshal Montgomery maintained that his September, 1944 plan for moving forward in strength would have finished the Germans that autumn; General Dwight Eisenhower was intent on a slower strategy. Montgomery continued to believe that the Ardennes battle need never have happened had he had his way.

Madman or genius?

Hitler's grand-slam in December, 1944, was to be a forced drive across Belgium to Antwerp. At first glance it seemed mad; but, as in all Hitler's schemes, it contained elements of genius. Antwerp was vital to the Allies in that it had a capacity, as a seaport, of supporting 50 divisions on a continuing basis. Its loss could have set back Eisenhower's plans by a year. And in that year, Hitler would bring in his V-weapons in force, and possibly the A-bomb which was almost ready. There was real method in his madness.

There was an additional prong to the Fuehrer's counter-offensive thrust. He knew there was schism in the Allied backrooms; he believed his move would lead to the break up of the alliance – a situation he would know brilliantly how to exploit. There was also the fact that Hitler had succeeded – against the will of his advisors – in defeating the French across this same territory in May 1940.

His generals believed he was being over-ambitious. They favoured a smaller slam in which they would cut behind the First Army and drive northwards, east of the Meuse. But Hitler had been right so often before, against all the odds, that once more his will prevailed. That he almost proved to be correct is one of the breath-taking aspects of this incredible Battle of the Bulge in the worst winter weather of the century.

He still had brilliant generals in the field –

notably Rundstedt, who was commander in chief on the Western Front, Model, Kruger, Manteuffel and Luttwitz – and they were not only loyal to him; they also had searing experience of fighting in the wildness of the eastern front to throw into the Ardennes counter-offensive.

Unbeknown to the 'all-seeing' dictator, however, there was a joker in his pack. The comparatively inexperienced General Sepp Dietrich, who was to command the four crack SS Divisions which would carry the main effort of the great offensive, was flawed. There were many reasons why Hitler's target was not achieved, and not least of them was the fact that Dietrich's Sixth Panzer Army failed against the American 5 Corps in the swamps and forest of the Hohe Venne.

Hitler misleads the Allies

Eisenhower's policy, at this moment in the war, was that the Germans should be allowed no respite to build up during the winter. In fact, he had greatly underestimated the true German strength. And Hitler had again fooled the Allies by establishing an entirely new system of command, with the division of the bulk of his forces in two: Guderian commanding some 200 divisions in the east and Rundstedt some 60 to 70 in the west. Reserves were to be drawn from the German 'home guard' – the Volkssturm. In all, this meant that Hitler had reconstituted an army at least equal in size to that with which he had begun the war.

Against this, Eisenhower's armies were spread over a wide front – thinly at some points, in order that they could be thick on the ground at positions of attack potential. As Hitler well knew, the Ardennes segment was but lightly garrisoned; the Americans regarded it as merely an outpost for the important line of the Meuse.

Panthers and Tigers

Hitler had another trump up his sleeve the Allies

Hitler's thrust through the Ardennes took fire-power – **top** *the Tiger II or King Tiger provided the punch with its 88 mm. main gun – and mobility –* **below** *German troops make their way through Belgium.*

1 Turret, 360° traverse
2 Commander's seat
3 Commander's periscope
4 Anti-aircraft machine-gun, MG34: 7.92 mm. (2,925 rounds)
5 Rear hatch
6 Ammunition for 88 mm. gun: 22 rounds
7 Maybach HL 230 V-12 engine: 690 bhp. Gears: 8 forward, 4 reverse
8 Engine-driven blower. Impels clean air through radiator
9 Radiators (on either side)
10 Fuel tank (one of seven). Total fuel carried: 210 gal (864 litres)
11 Side ammunition racks for 88 mm. (24 rounds each side)

12 Steel-tyred wheels (eight each side)
13 Track, $31\frac{1}{2}$in (79 cm.) wide
14 Forward bulkhead
15 Side armour, $3\frac{1}{8}$in (80.65 mm.) thick
16 Machine-gunner's seat
17 Machine-gun, 7.92 mm. MG34 (2,925 rounds)
18 Front wheel sprockets
19 Frontal armor, $3\frac{15}{16}$in – $5\frac{9}{10}$in (100 mm./150 mm.) thick
20 Disc-brake drum
21 88 mm. main armament, muzzle velocity 3,280 ft./sec.
22 Muzzle brake to reduce recoil
23 Shock absorber
24 Driver's seat
25 Spare 88 mm. ammunition

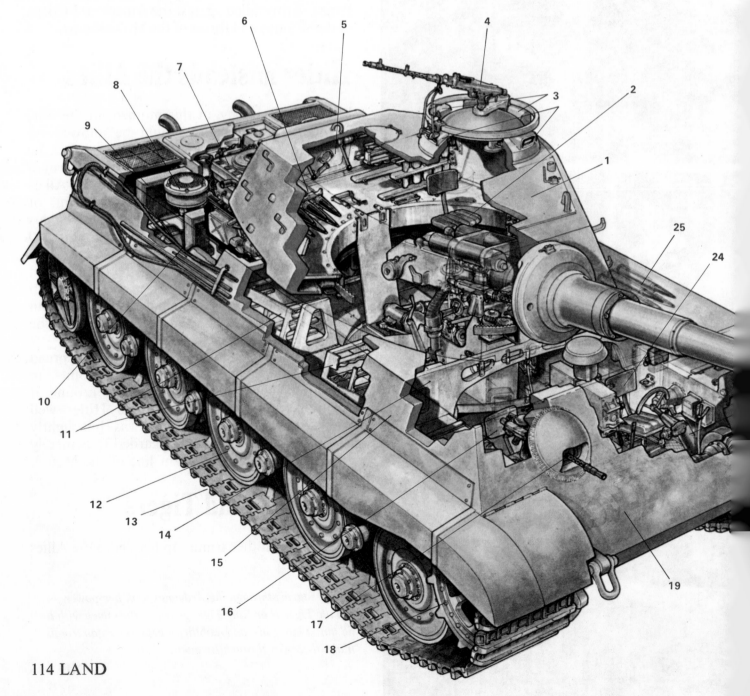

missed. The Sixth Panzer Army was being made ready for the counter-offensive so far from the front that Allied intelligence took it to be meant as a defensive reserve; and it was armed with the very latest heavy Panther and Tiger tanks.

This was the army Hitler believed could be driven straight through the Ardennes, across the Meuse, and across undefended country to Antwerp, cutting Eisenhower's forces in half on the way.

Rundstedt knew the way better than most. All his life he had studied the Ardennes, as one of the classic gateways into and out of Germany. And, in addition to the Sixth, Rundstedt planned also to commit the Fifth Panzer Army which was already in the line opposite Liege. These two would add up to the largest armoured spearhead the world had ever known, consisting of ten Panzer divisions, supported by 17 motorised divisions of the highest calibre, totalling at least 2,000 tanks and a quarter million men, in all.

Hitler had also ordered the use of two devices

The PzKw VI Tiger II – the Koenigstiger or King Tiger – commanded respect. The Americans thought it equivalent to four Shermans.

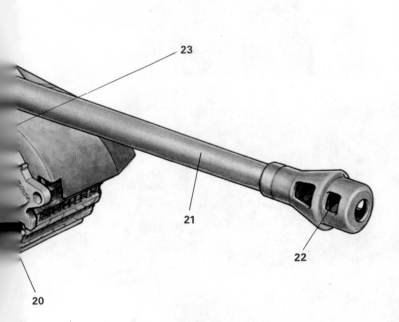

unheard of in modern warfare. One was a barrage of flying bombs; the other was an offensive recce brigade in American vehicles, some of its officers in American uniforms. These were 'suicide' troops whose do-or-die mission was to take and hold the Meuse bridges. The Luftwaffe had also regrouped, and was ordered to put up several thousand aircraft purely in tactical support.

The Allies hang fire

Eisenhower's winter offensive had got under way in November with a series of staggered attacks. There was to be no spearhead. One after another, the seven armies were to move on the Rhine in an endeavour to establish bridgeheads on the far side, and it was hoped that the Ruhr would be pierced. But, in most cases, the tanks were unable to follow the forward assault troops, and November's gains amounted to a few thousand yards at best. No bridgeheads were established. The Rhine continued to bar progress.

All Rundstedt needed now was a clear day, to begin the counter-offensive, followed immediately by the sort of bad weather that would keep the superior Allied air forces grounded.

Rundstedt strikes . . .

On the night of December 14 to 15, Rundstedt got what he wanted. The Fifth Panzer Army moved south to a point opposite Luxembourg; the Sixth took its place in the line. All was ready, and on December 16, in excellent conditions, both armies struck together on a front about 40 miles wide. The Bulge was about to be made.

Surprise was complete. The Allies were taken off balance. Half-a-dozen American divisions were rolled up, encircled, or over-run. Even army head-quarters were forced to pack up and run for it. Everyone had been thinking the war in Europe was virtually over and they had survived; now the situation was suddenly grave. Flying bombs were falling everywhere; German parachutists were landing in force behind the lines; for a few days chaos reigned. Not even SHAEF, supreme Allied head-quarters, had any clear idea of what was happening. A fog came to the aid of the Nazis, too, so that no Allied planes could take off for reconnaissance or defence.

... and Eisenhower counters

By December 18 things were totally out of control, and on December 19, with terrific rows going on among the Allies behind the scenes, Eisenhower – who had been made a five-star general three days before – took desperate measures.

He called in Montgomery to command all Allied land forces in the all-important northern shoulder, including the US First and Ninth Armies, and he moved Bradley to control the area south of a line from Givet to Prum, which gave him principally the Sixth Army Group. Bradley was to arrange a counter-attack through the so-called soft underbelly of the Bulge towards Houffalize; and Monty was to fight a defensive battle to hold the Germans away from the Meuse bridges at all costs.

There was little enough time for such counter-measures. It could not have been much more of a near thing. But the First American Army in the north had not panicked and was holding; and elsewhere – notably at Bastogne and St Vith – pockets or salients of American resistance were delaying German progress. Indeed this was perhaps Hitler's greatest miscalculation in planning his Ardennes drive. He had assumed the Americans would be easier to frighten than the British. He misread their 'sloppy' attitudes to discipline and their casual deportment.

Resourcefulness and stubborn bravery under attack were qualities he had not expected from the GIs. Their independence in 'going to business' for themselves, when out of touch with

headquarters upset Hitler's time-tables at several places in and around the Bulge. And these delays gave Montgomery and Bradley a few vital days to consolidate.

Montgomery quickly sent out 'spies' to gather information at all points of contact. In a matter of hours he was the only Allied officer 'in the picture'. He assessed the information and rightly guessed Rundstedt would attempt to wheel northwards and perform a left hook towards the Meuse near Liege. He set up a defensive corps in this path.

As the approach to the Meuse was held by the British and Americans, Eisenhower and Bradley hastily arranged a counter-attack from the south. They agreed there was only one man with the flexibility and charisma to get fresh troops into the line at Arlon. This was Eisenhower's long-time friend, the larger-than-life Lieutenant General George S. Patton Jnr., who tended to ride into battle on a cruiser tank like the US cavalryman he was at heart.

Patton steps in

Patton's Third Army had been poised for a major attack on the Saar just before Christmas. Asked on December 19 how quickly he could hand over and prepare to attack at the southern pimple of the bulge, he said 'Give me two days.'

'I'll agree to three or four, if that's possible,' said Eisenhower. 'Let's say not earlier than the 22nd and not later than the 23rd.'

'You're on!' said the irrepressible Patton, whose assessment of himself was that he was 'the ray of sunshine and the backslapper alike to superiors and to my men'.

It was no mean task to hand over, wheel his army through 90 degrees in a gigantic side-slip along wintry roads, and reorganize his elaborate communications system for the new attack all within 72 hours. But Patton did it. By December 22, he had three divisions fully prepared to take on the German Sixth Army – his 4th Armoured, with the 35th and 60th Infantry – as well as two more being readied, one armoured and one Infantry.

Left An American tank-destroyer with 105 mm. howitzer goes looking for a target. American resistance was the major factor in holding Hitler's first attacks.

The Bastards of Bastogne

The plan was to attack along a 30-mile front, with III Corps driving along the Arlon to Bastogne road to relieve the beleaguered 101st Airborne Division – symbol by that time of American toughness in battle – which had been holding on against all odds, in Bastogne supplied by air. Not without reasons these brave defenders called themselves the Battered Bastards of Bastogne.

This was in itself a swashbuckling mission in the Patton tradition. He reckoned he could pull it off in a couple of days and then push on up the bulge to link with the First Army.

But, for once, Patton's aims were beyond fulfilment. It should have gone well, for, on December 23, after 11 days in which all aircraft had been mainly grounded, the sun had come through, dispelling the milky fogs, and the combined fleets of the RAF and the Eighth

Below Lt.-Gen. Patton led the American counter-attack from the south. He visualized a grand drive through the Germans. The reality was tougher.

American Air Force were overhead with massive support.

Fighting was difficult and slow, with much close combat of the sort Patton liked least. And after two days of non-success on the ground, Patton had to tell Major General John Millicin, who was in charge of the III Corps thrust: 'There's too much piddling around. Press on and get the tanks through.' This was the 4th Armoured Division, the key to his plan for Bastogne.

On the afternoon of December 26, Christmas having been largely ignored, Patton's 4th Armoured broke through the minefields surrounding Bastogne and were greeted by General

Left Captured Germans in American uniforms, their job had been to hold the Meuse bridges.

Below The Sherman M4 with its 76 mm. armament became the main, well-liked Allied tank. Simple design and mass production put so many in the field that they over ran the technically superior King Tiger.

McAuliffe, commanding 101st Airborne with the laconic words: 'Gee, I am mighty glad to see you boys.'

At this moment, the Ardennes crisis could be said to have passed. Runsdtedt could no longer hope to plunge on to the Meuse and over it. He was being squeezed north and south. Progress was incredibly slow, with heavy losses in infantry. The weather closed in again and no longer could the Flying Fortresses be seen immensely high overhead, writing a message of hope in their con-trails. Men froze to death where they crouched; petrol and anti-freeze solidified; villages changed hands several times.

Montgomery and Bradley

With the turn of the year, both Montgomery and Bradley turned on the counter-counter-offensive in full force, both pressing towards Houffalize. Deep snowdrifts, icebound roads, belts of mine-fields and flying bombs gave the two-pronged contest the style of a tortoise race, with even do-or-die Patton's now-strengthened Third Army making less than a mile a day's progress. He had hoped to push on quickly after Bastogne, and send another three divisions on the road to Bonn. But he had underestimated the difficulty in cutting through the German Sixth Army. This period featured some of the grimmest fighting of the entire war.

But as January went on, the tortoises squeezed the Germans back to the original starting line in Germany, to the very temporary shelter of the Siegfried Line.

The war had come to the crunch. Allied combat soldiers had stood toe-to-toe with the Wehrmacht in comparable strength on a battle-ground chosen by Hitler and had finally broken the back of the Nazi all-conquering machine. In the Ardennes, Allied casualties had been about 80,000 to the Germans' 110,000.

There was still much fighting and dying to be done. But the result of the war had hung on the Battle of the Bulge. With that won, the outcome in Europe was no longer in doubt.

Hitler's plan to swoop through the Ardennes to the Channel ports ran foul of American resistance. Patton from the south and Montgomery and Bradley from the north gradually pushed the Germans back.

Battle of the Bulge

NETHERLANDS
Arnhem
Waal
Rhine
CANADIAN FIRST ARMY
BRITISH SECOND ARMY
Antwerp
Duisburg
U S NINTH ARMY
Düsseldorf
Brussels
Maas
Siegfried Line
Cologne
Planned German Advance
BELGIUM
GERMANY
Namur
U S FIRST ARMY
Sambre
Dinant
U S 8th CORPS
Meuse
Clervaux
Bastogne
Sedan
LUX
Echternach
Luxembourg
Trier
FRANCE
U S THIRD ARMY

U S FIRST ARMY
Malmédy
SIXTH PANZER ARMY
Dinant
FIFTH PANZER ARMY
Celles
Houffalize
SEVENTH PANZER ARMY
Bastogne
GENERAL PATTON AND U S THIRD ARMY

Furthest German Advance

Front Line after first Counter Attack

OPERATION COMMANDO

A true 'United Nations' took part in Operation Commando, an engagement in the Korean War during 1951 which involved bitter hand-to-hand-fighting against the Chinese by men from virtually every Commonwealth country supported by American tanks and aircraft.

Korea was the war with four million casualties and no victors. It went on for nearly three years, although the Communists began suing for peace before the first year's fighting was over.

The 38th parallel, which divided the totalitarian North Korean Democratic People's Republic from the West-orientated, free-wheeling, allegedly-democratic Republic of South Korea, was the Iron Curtain of the Far East.

The entire peninsula had been known historically as The Land of Morning Calm. But the morning of June 25, 1950 was pretty wild, as seven infantry divisions and one armoured division from the north invaded the comparatively-weak and defensive-minded south, using about 100 T34 Soviet tanks and 150 Yak fighters – supported by artillery and mortars in its aggressive probe.

More than a local war

But this was much more than a little local war. The country had been partitioned between the Russians and the Americans in 1945, as a military arrangement to facilitate the Japanese surrender. US occupation troops had been withdrawn for economic reasons, in 1949, but the Russians still ruled the northern roost.

NATO having blocked Soviet attempts to impose Marxist-Leninist beliefs on the countries of Europe, Stalin evidently thought that a swift take-over of South Korea, Hitler-fashion, might catch America looking the other way. He had no real faith in Mao and the Chinese Communists.

But President Truman responded swiftly, in a move he later described as 'my toughest decision'. Air and naval assistance was given at once, and the American-prodded UN Security Council recommended members to aid the southern Republic 'to repel the armed attack'. Led by America, 15 UN member countries would in due course send forces to the Republic of Korea, where a UN Command was set up. In due course, too, some incredible air battles would be fought there.

Troops from all over the Commonwealth combined in the Commonwealth Division that spearheaded Operation Commando – and saw some of the toughest fighting of the war. **Top left** *Canadians man a Vickers machine gun.* **Left** *A Sherman tank covers an infantry advance.*

As a kick-off, Truman ordered General Douglas MacArthur – then Supreme Allied Commander, based in Japan – to send US assault troops to South Korea. The American Eighth Army was assembled in record time and transported from Japan under General Walton Walker. Speed was of the essence, for by the first week in August, virtually all southern territory west of the Naktong River was in Communist hands.

MacArthur takes Inchon

MacArthur, now designated UN Commander, reacted with characteristic flamboyance. Napoleonically, he placed a US Marine division and an infantry division at Inchon, 200 miles behind the Communist lines, on September 15, 1950, whereupon the suddenly unsupported North Korean forces fled in disarray. Although the Russian tanks outgunned the American Shermans, the north's airforce could not last long against America's and Australia's flying power, while, around the peninsula, British and American warships tightened their stranglehold.

MacArthur then began a drive to Yalu, aimed at the 'liberation' of the north. At this point, Stalin considered intervention to save his 'satellite' state, but there was little doubt that this would have led to a Third World War. He dithered, and Communist China took over the situation instead.

Late in October, 1950, the first of 350,000 Chinese troops crossed the Yalu in support of North Korea, and these highly-trained, well-equipped and undeniably brave forces beat back MacArthur's 'home for Christmas' offensive towards the end of November. The Americans were pushed back from the Chongchong River, and the Chinese then moved freely south to the 38th parallel.

Riled at this set-back to his reputation as a fast positive operator, MacArthur wanted to reinforce and take the war offensively into Manchuria. Truman met British prime minister Clement Attlee in Washington just before Christmas. They decided the best plan was to defend the parallel and forget about unifying the two halves of Korea. Apart from everything else, America had already suffered more than 60,000 casualties, and the war was unpopular.

MacArthur was recalled to Washington, where

General Bradley told a joint session of Congress: 'Frankly, in the opinion of the Joint Chiefs of Staff, the MacArthur strategy would involve us in the wrong war, at the wrong place, at the wrong time, and with the wrong enemy. . . .'

General James Van Fleet took over as UN Commander in Korea. He had been a machine-gun captain in World War I, and had led an infantry regiment on D-day in the Second. Although he, too, was keen to push on to Manchuria, Van Fleet was bluntly told by General Ridgway – who had taken over from MacArthur in Tokyo – to carry out only 'limited offensives'.

Soon after this, the reinforced US forces were joined by a self-contained British brigade; Australia and New Zealand sent infantry and artillery; South Africa added a fighter squadron and Canada pledged to build up to a brigade. France, Belgium, Holland and India were also to play their parts.

The initial British forces – the 1st Middlesex and the 1st Argyll and Sutherland Highlanders – had arrived in August from Hong Kong, and were responsible for ten miles of the Allied line from the beginning of September. And when the redoubtable 3rd Royal Australian Regiment joined them, the three became the 27th British Commonwealth Brigade, under Brigadier B. A. Coad, fighting with the US 1st Cavalry Division.

The Chinese 'human wave'

Early in 1951, the front line moved up and down the peninsula as the weight of numbers engaged increased, first on one side and then on the other. In particular, the American and British forces just south of the 38th parallel inflicted incredibly heavy casualties on the fanatical Chinese motorized infantry which were attempting to break through to the south coast. Two later drives by the Chinese in April and May were halted by the superiority of American fire-power, on or near the parallel. The May battle was particularly bloody, and led to a Communist withdrawal for regrouping.

The Chinese had been blandly sacrificing themselves in apparently-endless waves – a bafflingly heartless technique in battle which became known as the 'human sea' or 'tidal wave' tactic. They had ceased publication of casualty figures, and whether these were ever made known to the Chinese people is doubtful.

Britain and America . . .

In truth, the main spring offensive of 1951 from the north was largely fought and won by the 27th (Commonwealth) Brigade and the 29th British Brigade. These had worked out defensive drills, based on barbed wire, machine guns and dugouts, on which the Communists died like lemmings. This succeeded, in contrast to the American 'butt out' technique. But in due course, the Communists brought up bangalore torpedoes and pole charges to blast through the wire, so that the men of the two Commonwealth brigades had literally to wait till they saw the whites of the enemies' eyes.

. . . Australia and Canada

From these brigades, two battalions were singled out to receive a Presidential Citation from Truman. Only one other unit was so honoured at this stage of the Korean war – 'A' Company, 72 US Heavy Tank Battalion.

This was the beginning of the end for Communist ambitions in the area in that phase of the Cold War. From July, apparently interminable negotiations proceeded at Kaesong and Panmunjom.

At this period, the UN Line ran from a point on the west coast (about 20 miles south of the 38th parallel) north-eastwards to the east coast, approximately 20 miles north of the parallel, which it cut some 40 miles north-east of Seoul. It was to remain a stable line throughout the summer.

In July, 1951, the 27th Commonwealth Brigade became part of the 1st Commonwealth Division, when the American-trained 25th Canadian Brigade arrived at the front. The third segment of the division was Brigadier Tom Brodie's experienced 29th Brigade. This consisted of the 8th King's Royal Irish Hussars, the Belgian Battalion, the 16th and 45th Field Regiments, Royal New Zealand Artillery, and the 170th Mortar Battery. All were experienced in Korean fighting. The 60th Indian Field Ambulance was

A machine-gunner keeps watch over terrain typical of the hill country north of the River Imjin where Operation Commando took place.

also to be an important part of the division. The Argylls and the Middlesex had by now been relieved by the 1st King's Own Scottish Borderers, and the 1st King's Shropshire Light Infantry.

All in all, this was the first time in history that British, Australian, Canadian, Indian and New Zealand troops had been integrated in a combat division under a unified command.

The division also became, to a large measure, independent of the Americans. Up to this point the various Commonwealth units had been under American corps commanders, and the tendency had been to employ them as a sort of reliable stop-gap in an emergency.

The 1st Commonwealth Division was under the command of Major General A. J. H. 'Gentleman Jim' Cassells, a Seaforth Highlander and a highly experienced tactician who had commanded the 51st Highland Division in Europe in in World War II when in his thirties. Except for

Below A Bren gun team prepares to move out.

Opposite Australian troops 'brew up'. With the Scots, Australians saw one of the wildest day's fighting of the Korean War when they helped take Hill 355 and hold it against wild Chinese counter-attacks.

one Canadian, the divisional commanders were British. Regimental commanders included Lieutenant Colonel Hasset, an Australian, and Lieutenant Colonel Young, a New Zealander.

Lice and rats

There being no real fighting in August, the Commonwealth Division was exercised in the line by General Cassells. They were holding a sequence of cratered hills facing the Imjin River. These were infested by lice and by rats; they were hot by day and bitterly cold by night. But the 'men of Empire' made themselves as comfortable as they could by improvisation and 'kept their powder dry'.

The Commonwealth Division faced the 192nd Chinese Division, in their olive-green quilted uniforms, across the hills of what was known as the Kansas Line, south of the Widgeon Crossing on the Imjin River. Their neighbours were the US 1st Corps, and the Chinese 192nd had as their neighbours, their 190th and 191st Divisions.

The Chinese forward elements were about two miles north of the river. Their main defences were some 7,000 yards to the rear, which meant an unusually wide belt of no-man's-land.

In the quiet before the storm, the left of the

Commonwealth front was held by British infantry battalions and the right by Australian infantry. The 25th Canadians were held in reserve. To left and right of the Commonwealth troops were the 1st South Korean Division and the 1st US Cavalry Division respectively.

Early in September, spearheaded by the 3rd Battalion, Royal Australian Regiment (regarded by many as the finest fighting infantry in Korea), the Commonwealth force launched a probing raid across the Imjin against light opposition. A few Chinese prisoners were taken and interrogated, but little information about the enemy was obtained. When no counter-attack developed, a bridgehead was formed and within a few days the entire division was fed through to the far bank of the river without further fighting. This permitted a new defensive line to be established some 6,000 yards north of the river, in the Mison Myor area.

In the first week of October, General Van Fleet, commanding US Eighth Army, was given permission by Ridgway to launch a limited offensive. If successful, the advance was to be kept to about five miles, where the hills would offer better surveillance over the Chinese front and its supply lines. The Commonwealth Division was to be used, in its first ever major attack against defended positions, to facilitate the advance of the US 1st Corps.

The truce talks had been on and off several times. Now M. Malik, the Soviet UN representative, was apparently offering peace overtures but in such a double-talking way that a rap on Chinese knuckles was generally considered to be timely.

Operation Commando begins

The Commonwealth attack was given the code name Operation Commando. It was planned to

be carried out in three stages. The first was to be an attack on the right by the 28th Commonwealth Infantry Brigade (the new name of the original 27th) to secure the dominant feature known as Hill 355, together with adjoining hills. The second move was to be an advance on day two by the 25th Canadian Infantry Brigade on the left to capture and hold a line of high ground about two miles ahead of their position. Third move was to be the exploitation to the divisional line by the Canadian Brigade and the Commonwealth Brigade on the right.

First Battalion King's Own Scottish Borderers led the 28th into the attack at 3 a.m. on October 2, with the Australian infantrymen and the 1st King's Shropshire Light Infantry in support. The Royal Northumberland Fusiliers were also in attendance, having been brought in as specialists to carry out the separate task of capturing Hill 217, which adjoined Hill 355.

Yet a third hill in the neighbourhood, numbered 317, was to be assaulted by the 3rd Battalion Royal Australian Regiment.

Bayonets and bagpipes

Surprise was better than expected in the cold dark of the October morning. The KOSB had advanced nearly a mile, and had almost reached the first outposts before the Chinese had any inkling of what was afoot. Just before dawn, the Communists opened up with artillery, mortar and machine gun fire, and the Scots had to go to ground. They did this in the hillocks preceding the strong defensive positions the Chinese were holding along and atop steep hills in their forward positions.

The going then became extremely hard for the Borderers and the Shropshires who had joined them. But, meanwhile, the Australians had succeeded in storming and capturing a fortified elevation to the right of the divisional front and they were able to give covering fire as the KOSB again advanced.

On the second day, the Australians and the

Top A British Centurion tank lies in wait.

Bottom American infantry watch as UN troops drop white phosphorus on Communist-held areas. American support was essential to Operation Commando.

Scots crept forward, step by step, under withering Chinese fire. Using grenades and small-arms, with tenacious courage and flair, they took another Chinese strongpoint, going in with the bayonet in the final charge.

As the Australians again paused to give cover, the Border regiment advanced, led by a piper, on the afternoon of the second day and took the all-important Hill 355.

It was one of the wildest days of the entire Korean war. The Chinese now realized the scope and scale of the Commonwealth attack. They opened up barrage after barrage until the hills were pock-marked with shell-craters. Overhead Migs swarmed in, to be taken in combat by the Royal South African Air Force, while American fighter-bombers pounded the Communist positions with rockets a mere few hundred yards ahead of the British and Australian infantry.

A score or so of powerful T34 tanks then appeared on the right flank, where they were challenged to battle by the 75 mm guns of the American cavalry's Shermans, and by New Zealand anti-tank six-pounders.

The Communists then employed their latest weapon. This was a network of huge loudspeakers which roared out recorded messages in broken English, *à la* Goebbels, ludicrously interspersing such commands as 'Jocks go home!' with Communist 'home truths' on the decadence of the West.

By the time the Fusiliers had fought their way yard by yard up the steep slopes of Hill 217 and were engaged in hand-to-hand clearing operations on the top, at sundown on October 4, it was estimated that nearly 1,000 mortar bombs and 15,000 shells had fallen in the contested areas of no-man's land that day. And, in the same evening, a suicide regiment of Chinese commandos swarmed up the hill and re-took it from the Geordie fusiliers. Twice more that night Hill 217 changed hands and mounds of bodies littered its faces.

Hill 317, toughest of all

The next morning, just before dawn, the Australians went for Hill 317. This was the toughest of the three objectives physically, for it was a pyramid in shape and could only be climbed on hands and knees.

Nineteen Chinese machine-guns nests covered

the Australian attack from the east. These were pounded by the RSAF and the American Air Force, but they were so well entrenched they survived. Australian progress was snail-slow. By dusk they were close enough to call up an artillery barrage and follow through with a bayonet attack. Thus they succeeded in mounting the lower defences of the hill, killing 58 Chinese in the process and taking 70 prisoners. There they remained for the night.

The following dawn saw the Australians moving on to a strong point higher up the feature, known as The Hinge. It was a key to the hill's conquest. Against deadly fire, they took The Hinge by 11 a.m. and held it all day despite a sequence of desperate counter-attacks.

In the late evening the feature was lit by a tremendous Chinese mortar and artillery bombardment. Even before the last shells had landed, wave after wave of Chinese assault troops had followed in, but the Aussies decimated them without faltering.

All night thereafter 'goon' patrols tried to creep up on the Allied positions, but flares and good marksmanship defeated each move. At 6 a.m., the Chinese retreated, taking with them some hundreds of their dead and wounded.

All three aims had been achieved. General Van Fleet sent unstinted congratulations to the Commonwealth Division which had welded itself so remarkably into a brave and efficient fighting unit in a very short time.

'Their sheer guts were beyond belief,' said Lt. Col. F. G. Hassett, who had commanded the Australians. He was speaking of the Scots and English as well as of his fellow-countrymen.

The Commonwealth had lost 58 killed and 262 wounded. Chinese casualities were five times as heavy but, more than that, they had suffered the equivalent of losing face. Thereafter stalemate prevailed, with but occasional flashes of cut-and-thrust until the much-delayed truce was signed on July 27, 1953. North and South Korea resumed the territories they had held three years before and settled down to lick unnecessary wounds, inflicted by the Great Powers, which would never entirely heal.

Operation Commando was a limited engagement in an indeterminate war. The aim was to stabilize the front line until Communists and UN reached a political settlement.

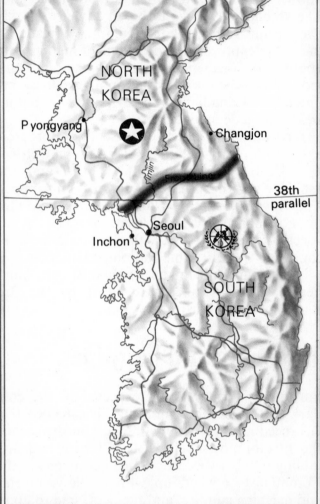

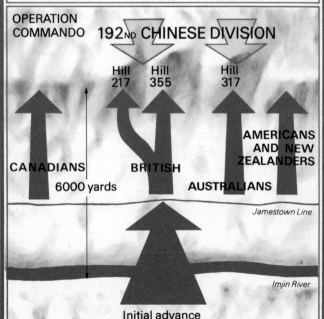